FOR ORGANS, PIANOS & ELECTRONIC KEYBOARDS

266

 LATIN HITS

ISBN 978-0-7935-8941-8

HAL•LEONARD®
CORPORATION

7777 W. BLUEMOUND RD. P.O. BOX 13819 MILWAUKEE, WI 53213

E-Z PLAY ® TODAY Music Notation © 1975 by HAL LEONARD CORPORATION

Visit Hal Leonard Online at
www.halleonard.com

LATIN HITS

CONTENTS

Adios

Registration 2
Rhythm: Rhumba or Latin

English Words by Eddie Woods
Spanish Translation and Music by Enric Madriguera

A - diós, _____
A - diós, _____

_____ In leav - ing you, it grieves me to say A -
_____ *Me voy lin - da mo - re - na le - jos de*

diós. _____
ti _____

I'll be so lone - ly,
El al - ma he - cha una

for you on - ly I sigh and cry my A -
pe - na por que al par - tir te - mo que tu ol -

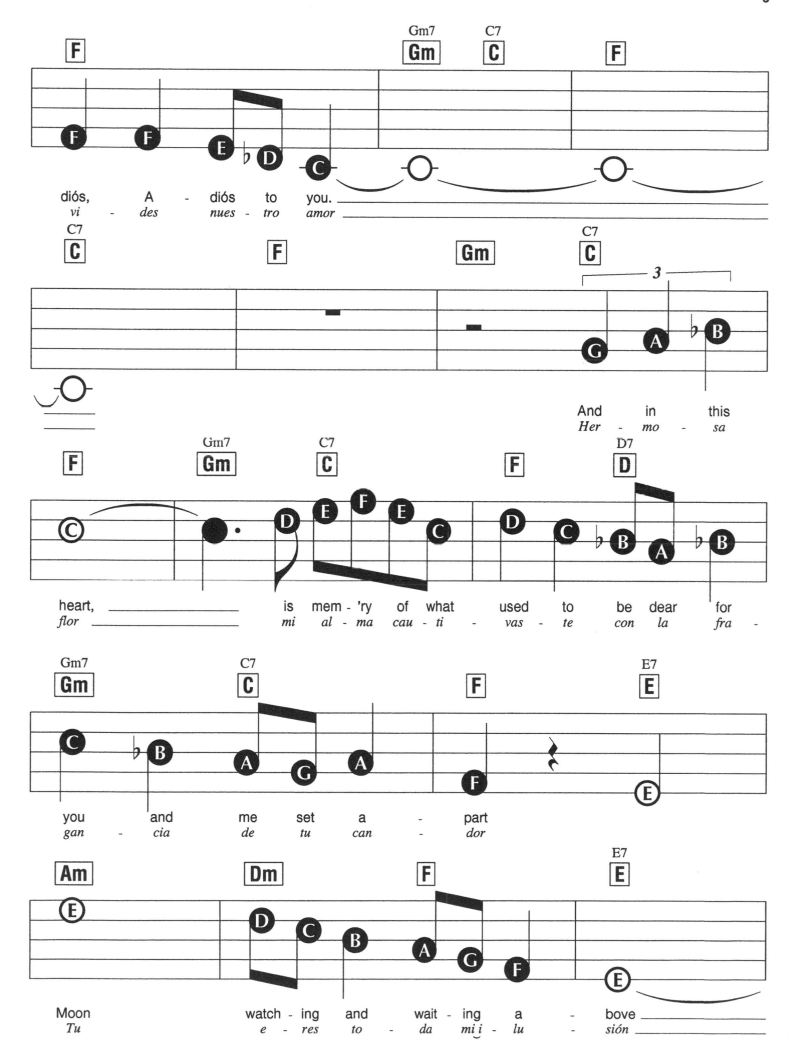

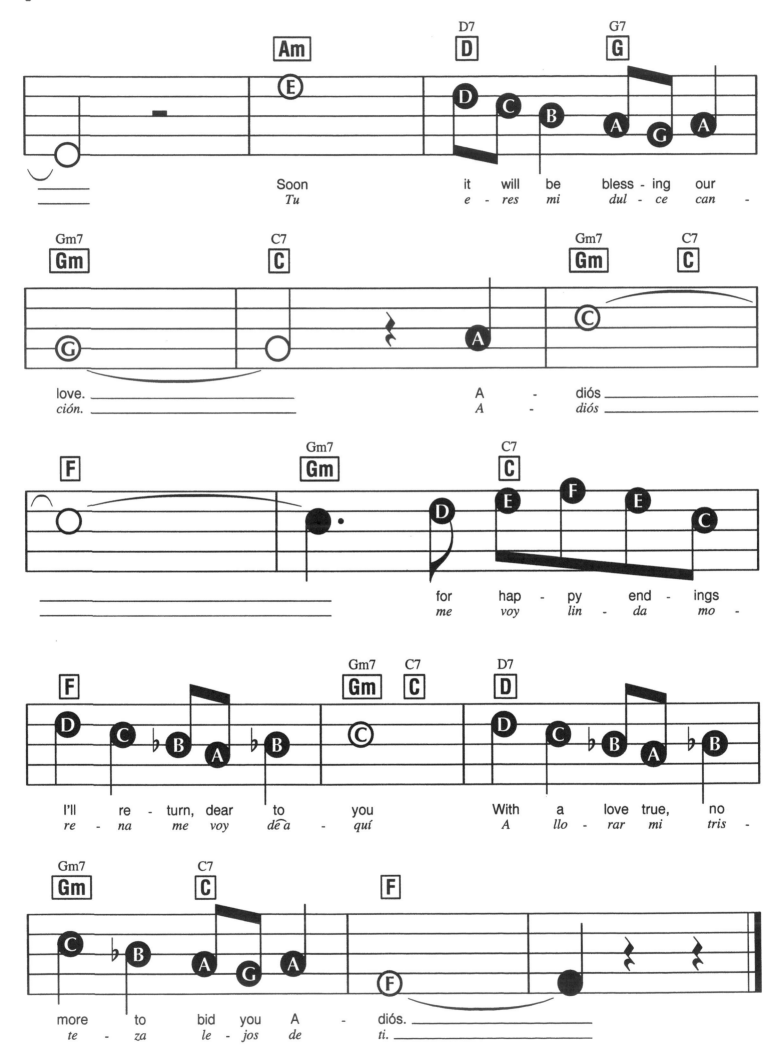

Always In My Heart
(Siempre En Mi Corazon)

English Words by Kim Gannon
Original Words and Music by Ernesto Lecuona

Registration 4
Rhythm: Rhumba or Latin

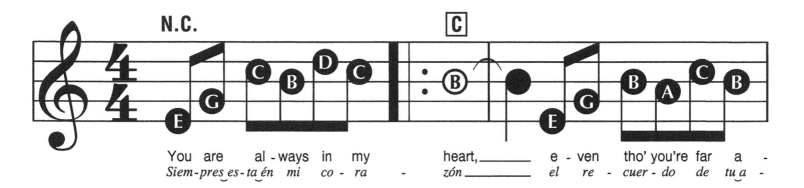

You are al-ways in my heart,_____ e-ven tho' you're far a-
Siem-pres es-ta én mi co-ra - *zón* _____ *el re-cuer-do de tu a-*

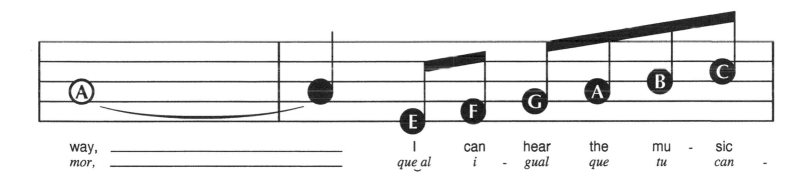

way, _____ I can hear the mu - sic
mor, _____ *que al i - gual que tu can-*

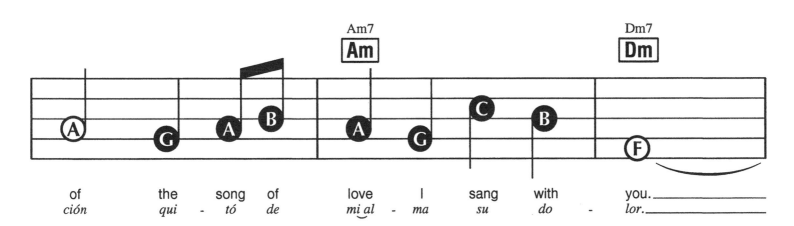

of the song of love I sang with you._____
ción qui - tó de mi al - ma su do - lor. _____

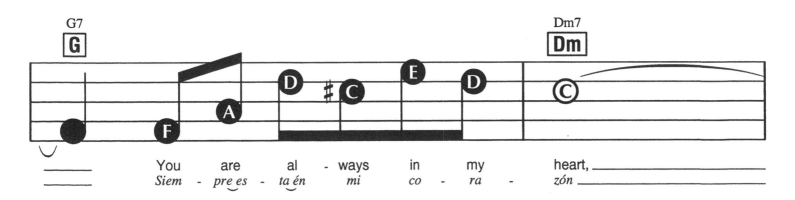

You are al - ways in my heart,_____
Siem - pre es-ta én mi co-ra - zón _____

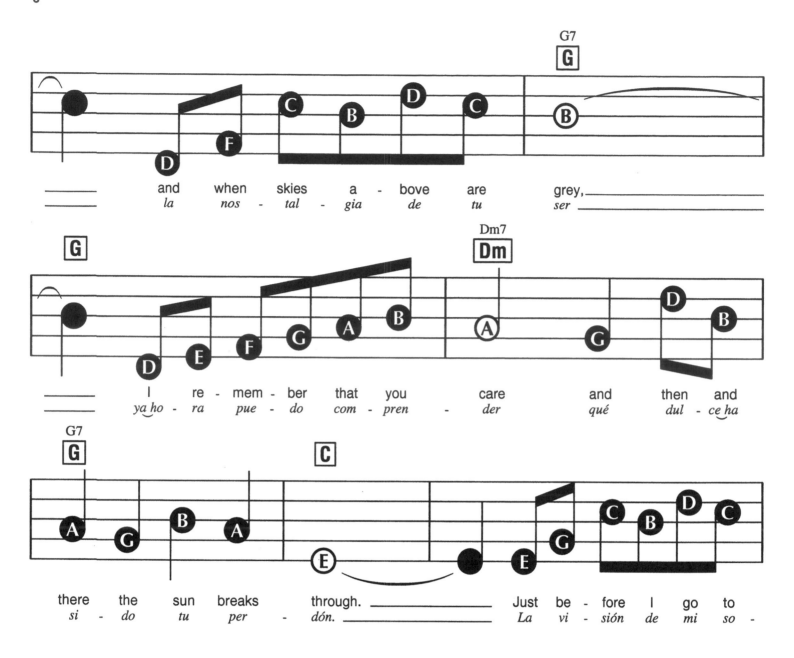

G7 G

and when skies a - bove are grey,_____
la nos - tal - gia de tu ser

G Dm7 Dm

_____ I re - mem - ber that you care and then and
ya ho - ra pue - do com - pren - der qué dul - ce ha

G7 C

there the sun breaks through._____ Just be - fore I go to
si - do tu per - dón._____ La vi - sión de mi so -

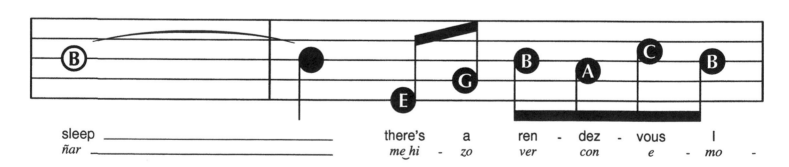

sleep_____ there's a ren - dez - vous I
ñar_____ me hi - zo ver con e - mo -

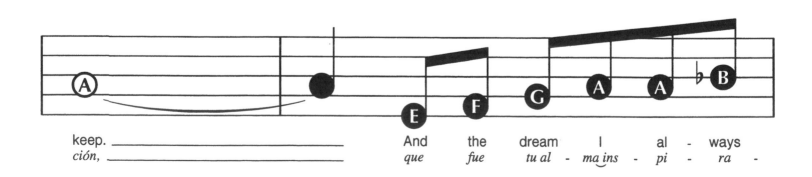

keep._____ And the dream I al - ways
ción,_____ que fue tu al - ma ins - pi - ra -

Blame It on the Bossa Nova

Registration 4
Rhythm: Latin or Bossa Nova

Words and Music by Barry Mann
and Cynthia Weil

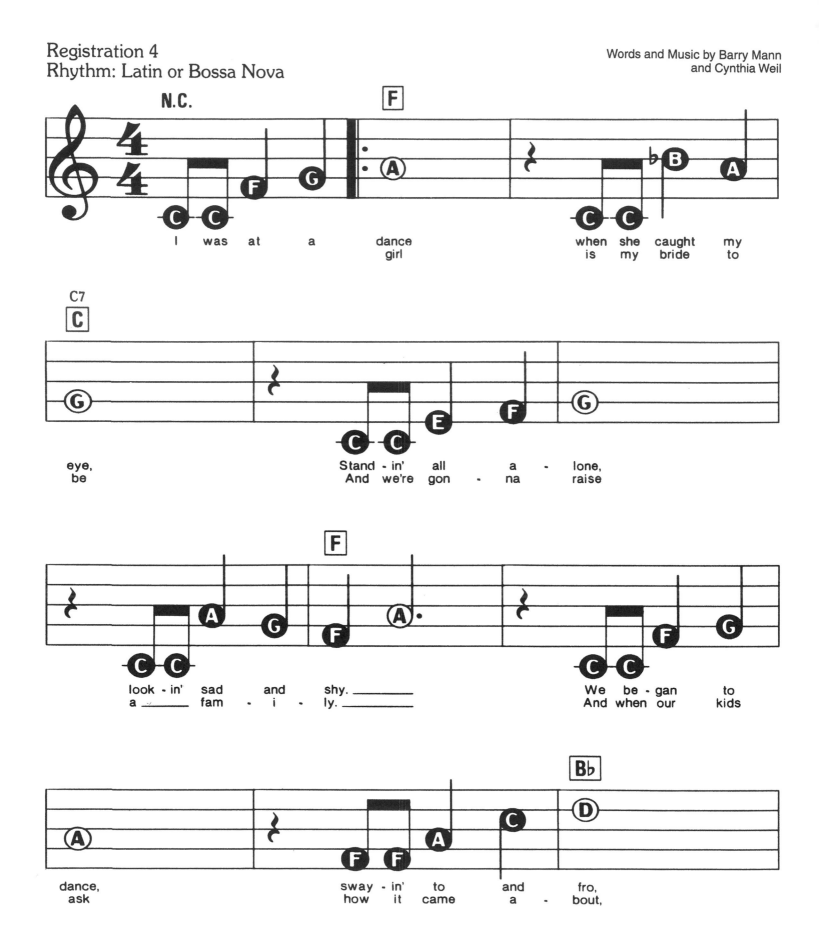

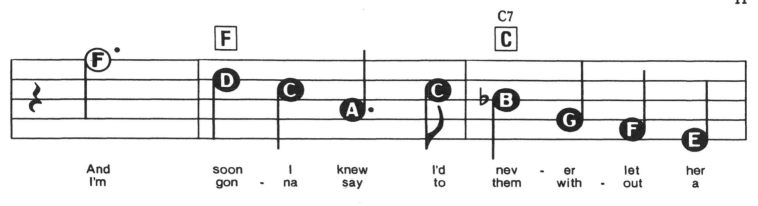

And soon I knew I'd nev - er let her
I'm gon - na say to them with - out a

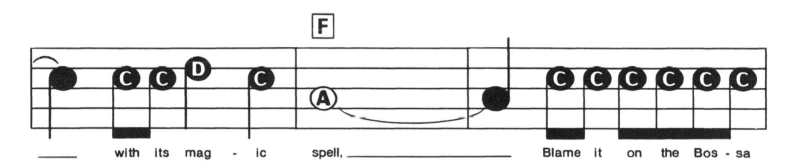

go. _____ Blame it on the Bos - sa No - va _____
doubt. _____

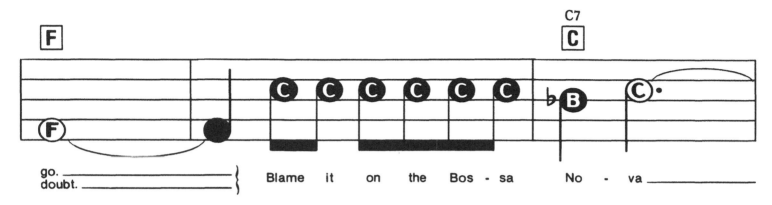

_____ with its mag - ic spell, _____ Blame it on the Bos - sa

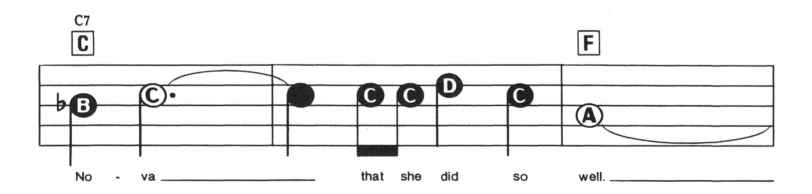

No - va _____ that she did so well. _____

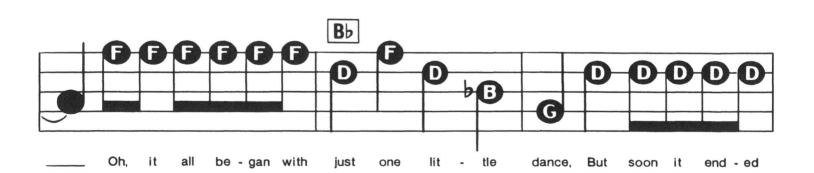

_____ Oh, it all be - gan with just one lit - tle dance, But soon it end - ed

12

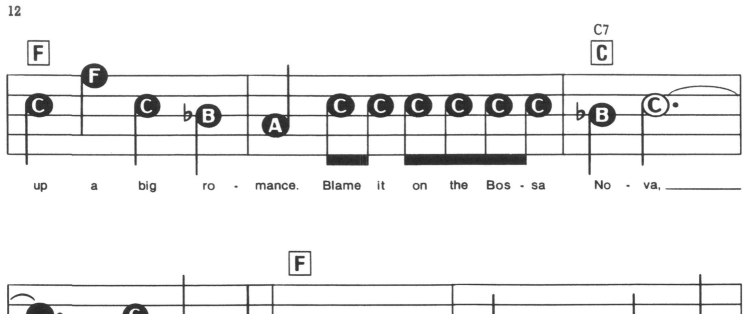

up a big ro - mance. Blame it on the Bos - sa No - va, _____

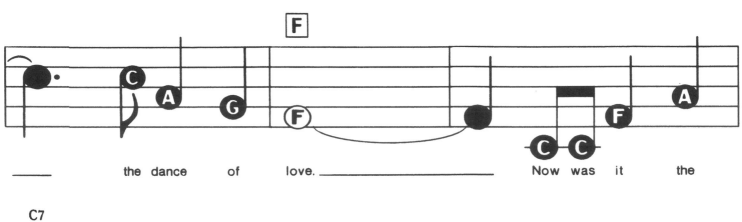

_____ the dance of love. _____ Now was it the

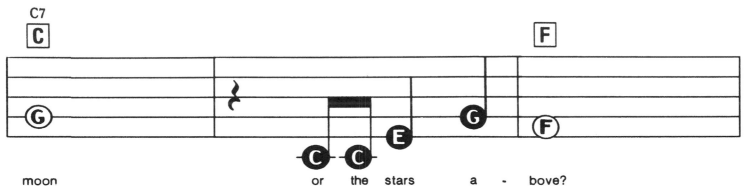

moon or the stars a - bove?

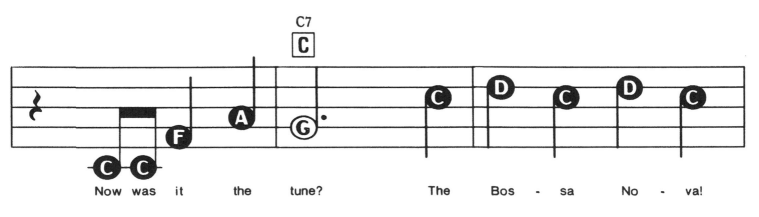

Now was it the tune? The Bos - sa No - va!

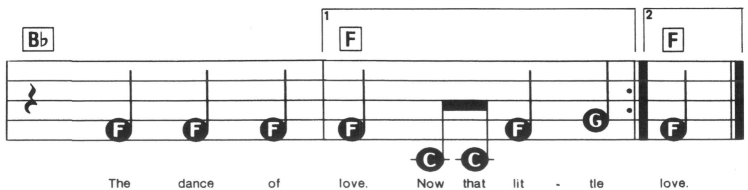

The dance of love. Now that lit - tle love.

Cherry Pink and Apple Blossom White

from UNDERWATER

Registration 9
Rhythm: Latin or Rhumba

French Words by Jacques Larue
English Words by Mack David
Music by Louiguy

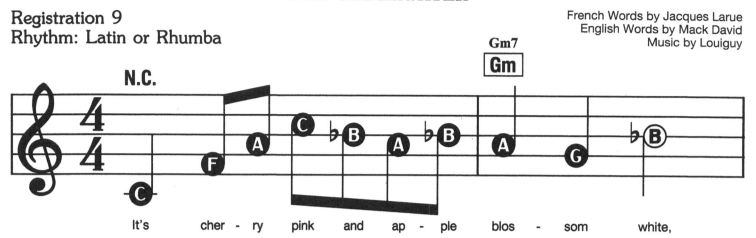

It's cher - ry pink and ap - ple blos - som white,

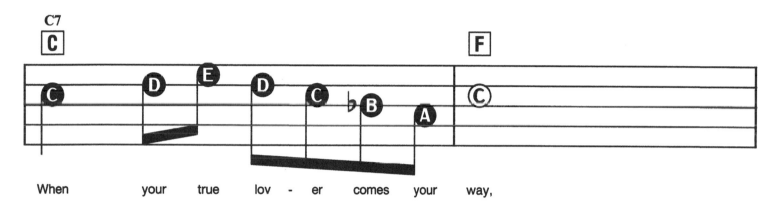

When your true lov - er comes your way,

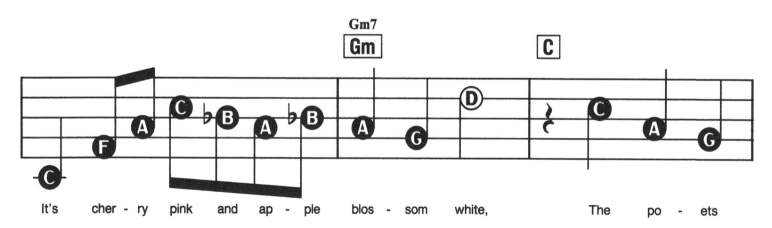

It's cher - ry pink and ap - ple blos - som white, The po - ets

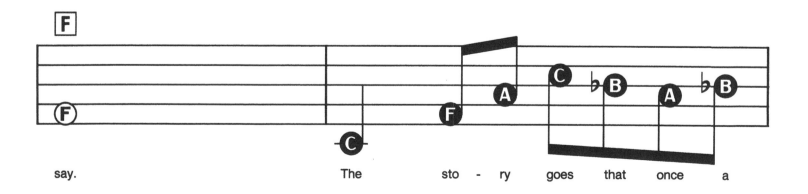

say. The sto - ry goes that once a

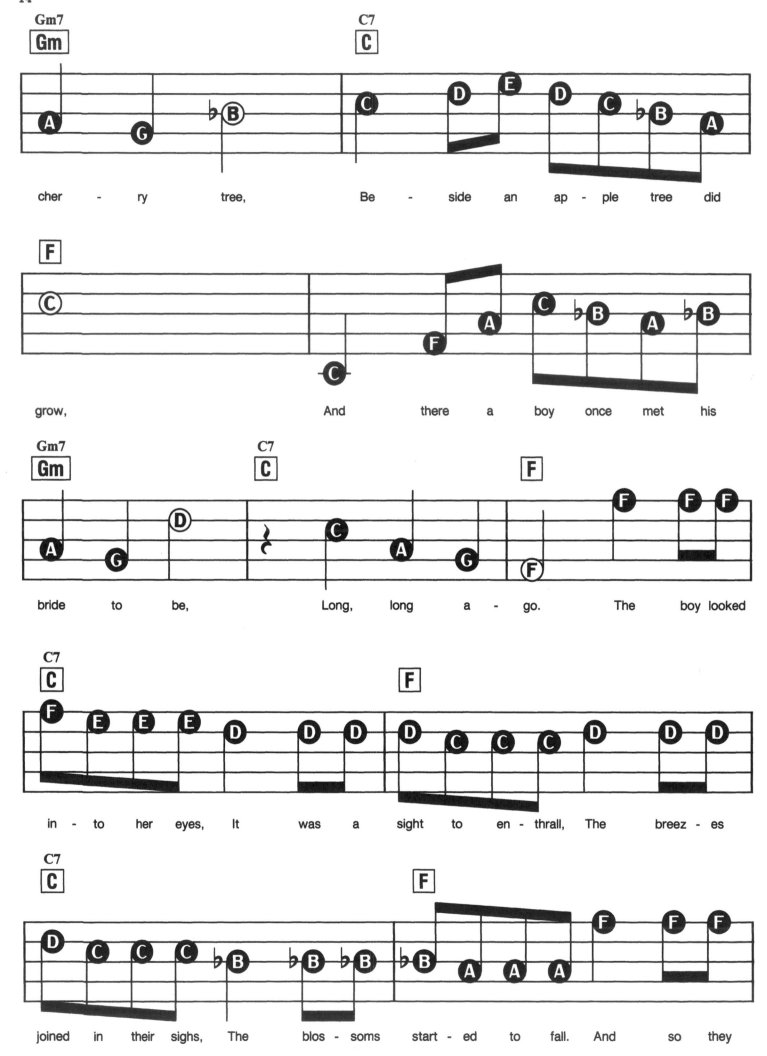

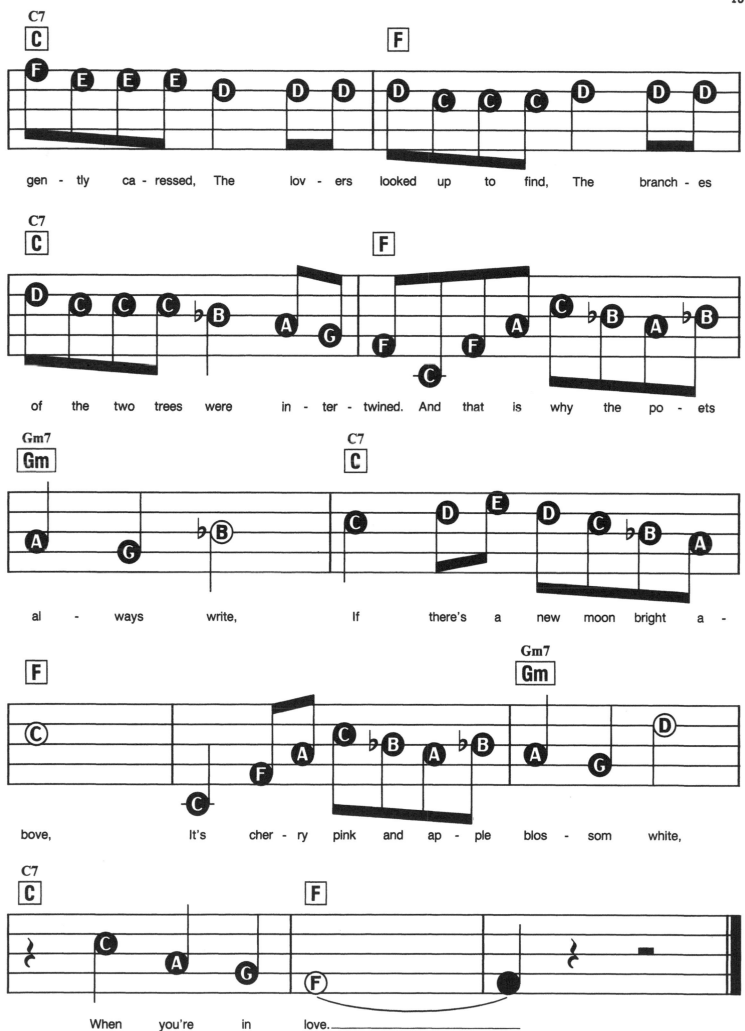

Brazil

Registration 4
Rhythm: Samba or Latin

Words and Music by S.K. Russell
and Ary Barroso

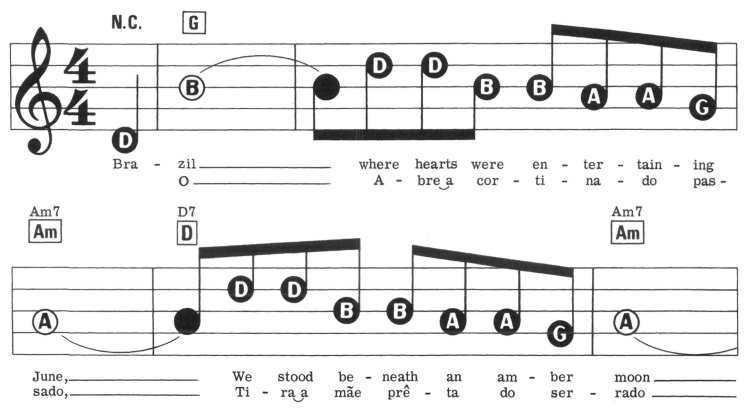

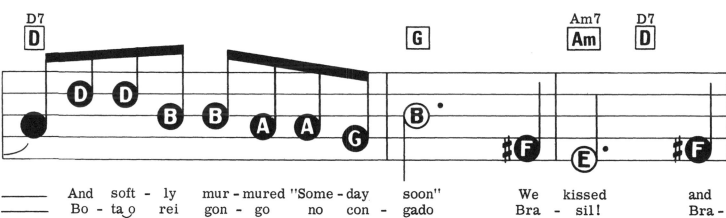

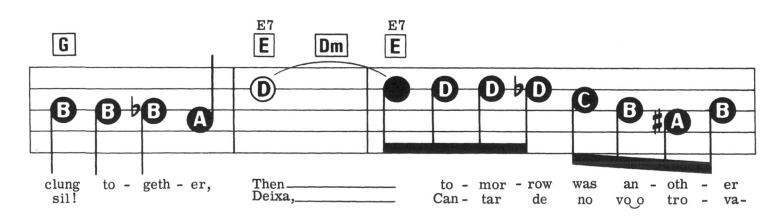

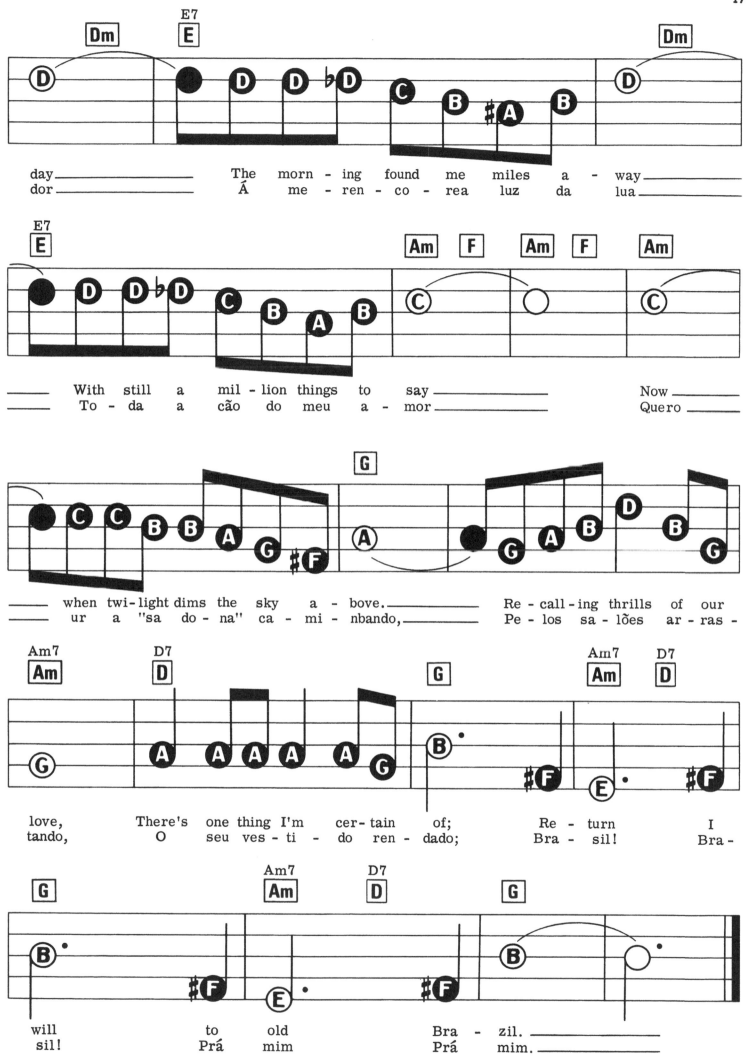

Don't Cry for Me Argentina
from EVITA

Registration 9
Rhythm: Tango or Latin

Words by Tim Rice
Music by Andrew Lloyd Webber

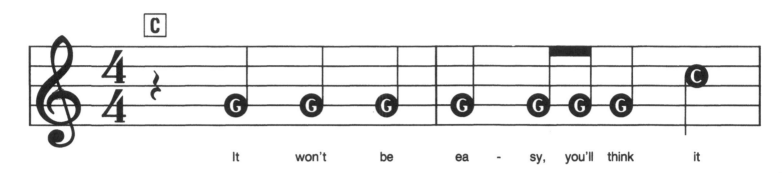

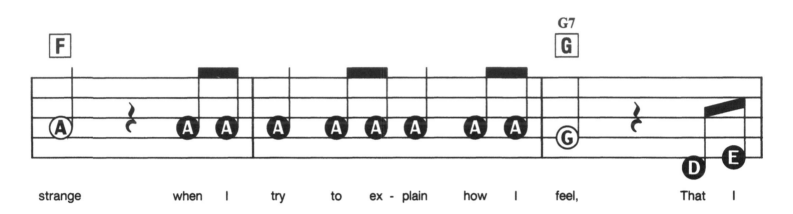

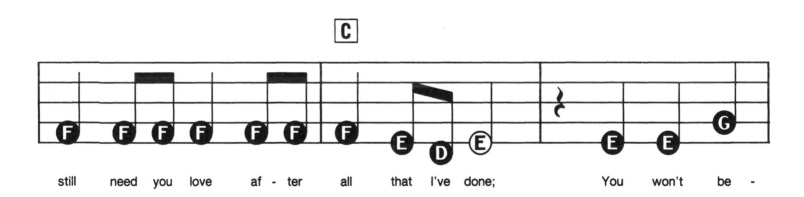

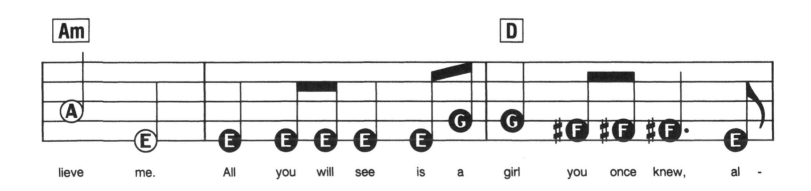

MCA music publishing

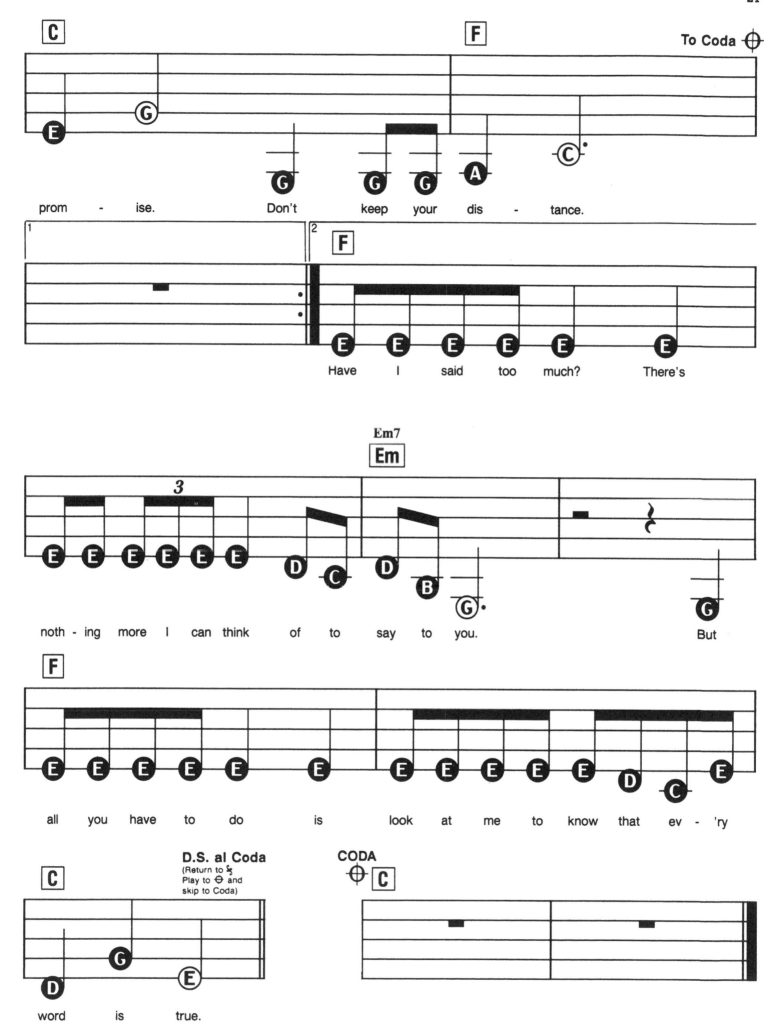

Frenesi

Registration 2
Rhythm: Rhumba or Latin

Words and Music by
Alberto Dominguez

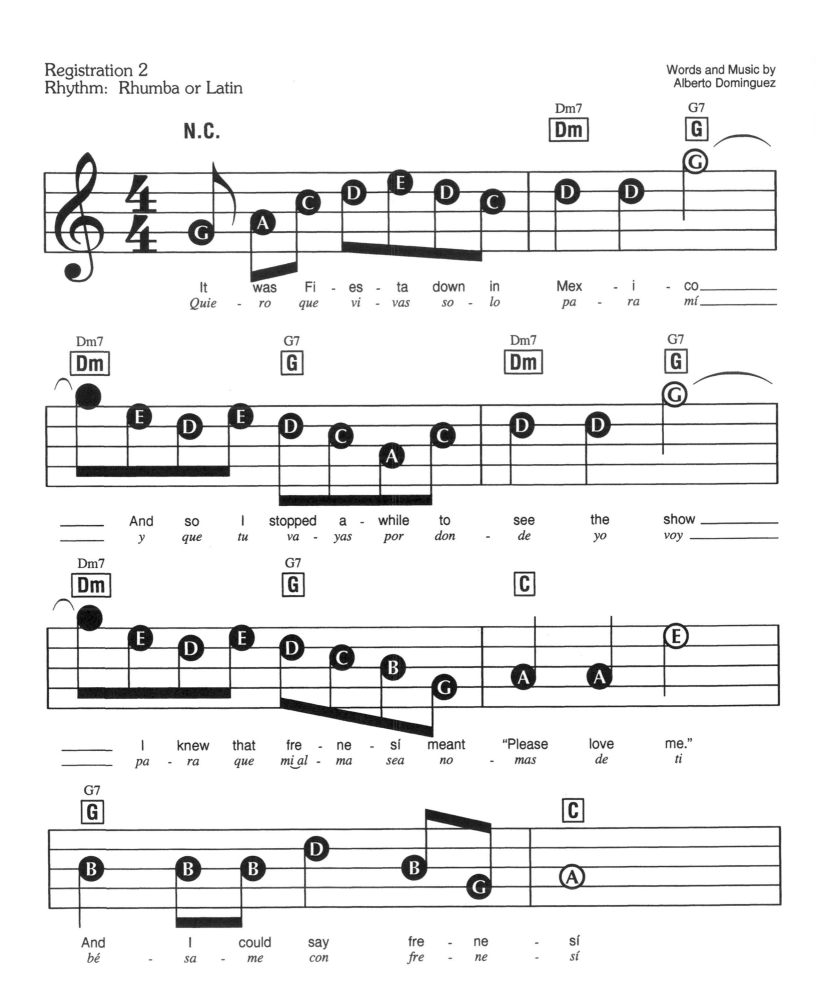

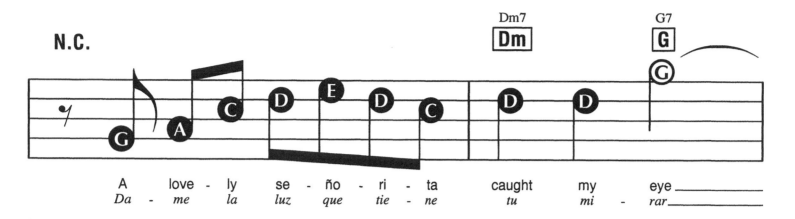

A love - ly se - ño - ri - ta caught my eye _____
Da - me la luz que tie - ne tu mi - rar_____

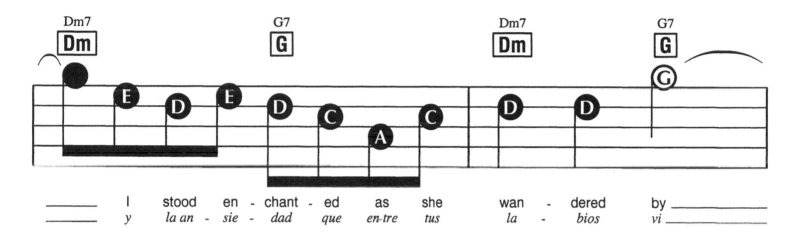

_____ I stood en - chant - ed as she wan - dered by _____
_____ y la an - sie - dad que en-tre tus la - bios vi_____

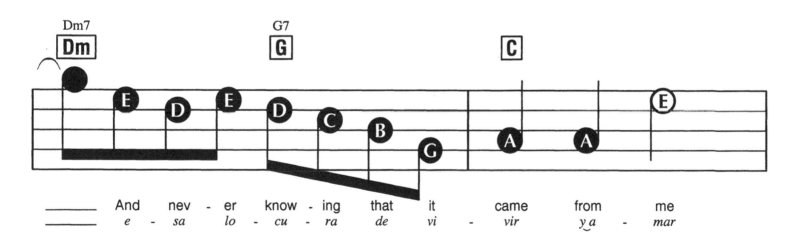

_____ And nev - er know - ing that it came from me
_____ e - sa lo - cu - ra de vi - vir y a - mar

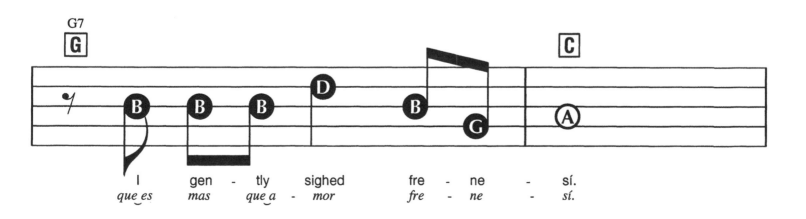

I gen - tly sighed fre - ne - sí.
que es mas que a - mor fre - ne - sí.

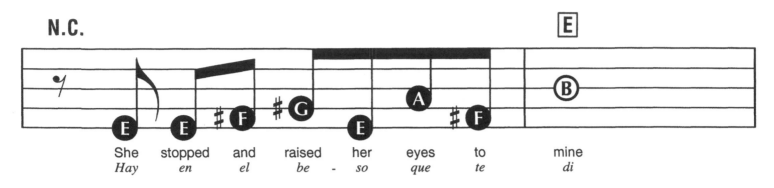

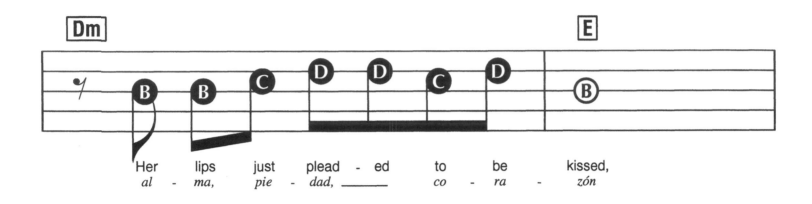

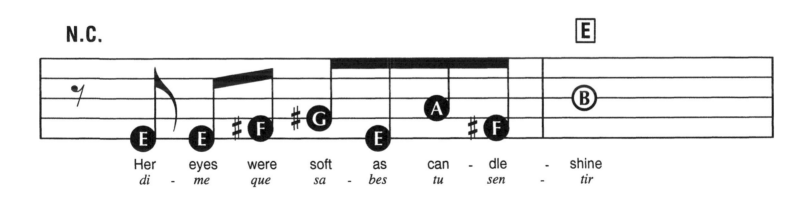

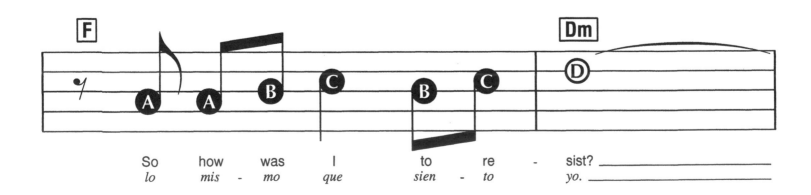

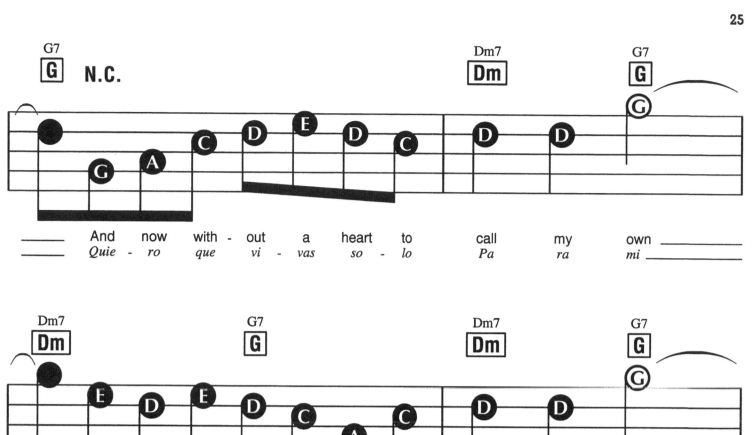

And now with-out a heart to call my own _____
Quie - ro que vi - vas so - lo Pa ra mi _____

A great - er hap - pi - ness I've nev - er known _____
y que tu va - yas por don - de yo voy

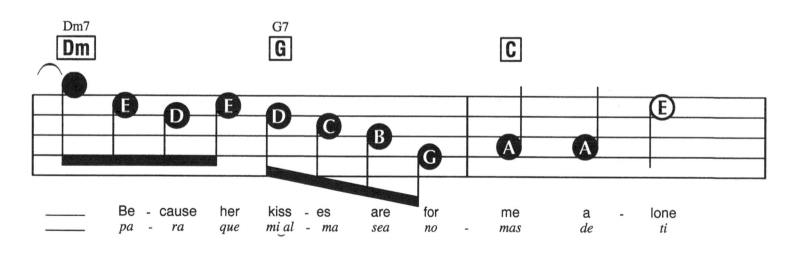

Be - cause her kiss - es are for me a - lone
pa - ra que mi al - ma sea no - mas de ti

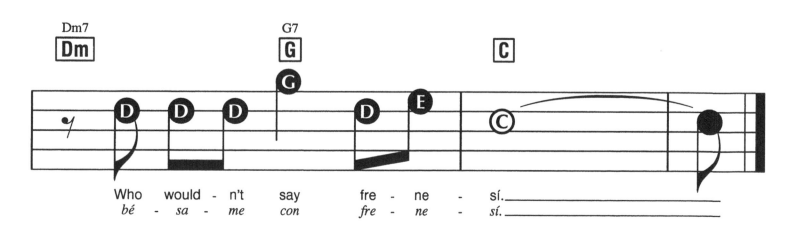

Who would -n't say fre - ne - sí._____
bé - sa - me con fre - ne - sí._____

Guantanamera

Original Words and Music by
Jose Fernandez Diaz (Joseito Fernandez)
Music adaptation by Pete Seeger
Lyric adaptation by Hector Angulo, based on a poem by Jose Marti

Registration 7
Rhythm: Bossa Nova

27

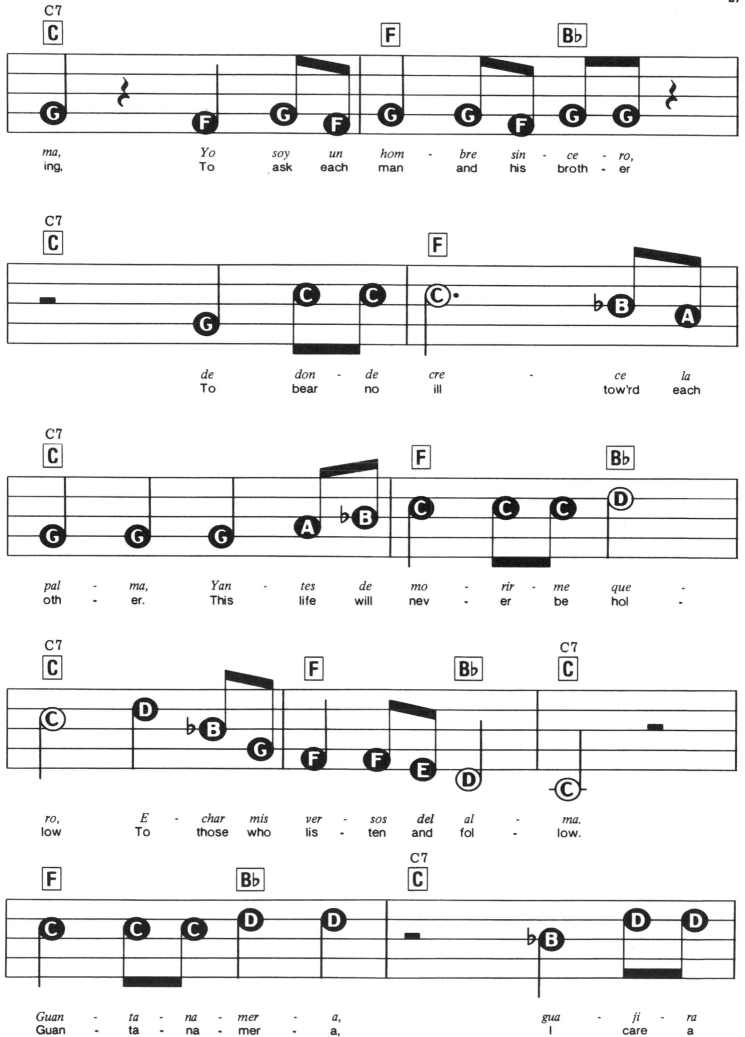

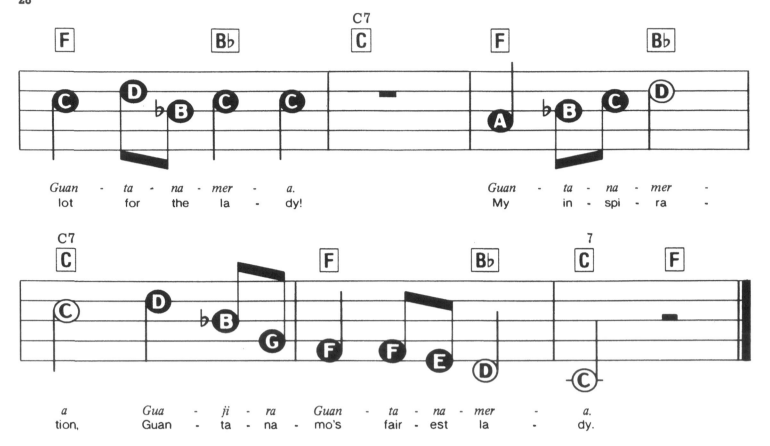

Guan - ta - na - mer - a.
lot for the la - dy!

Guan - ta - na - mer -
My in - spi - ra -

a Gua - ji - ra Guan - ta - na - mer - a.
tion, Guan - ta - na - mo's fair - est la - dy.

Spanish verses

1. *Yo say un hombre sincero,*
De donde crece la palma,
Yantes de morirme quiero,
Echar mis versos del alma.

2. *Mi verso es de un verde claro,*
Y de un carmin encendido,
Mi verso es un cierro herido,
Que busca en el monte amparo.

3. *Con los pobres de la tierra,*
Quiero yo mi suerie echar,
El arroyo de la sierra,
Me complace mas que el mar.

NOTE - Repeat chorus after
each of the above verses.

Literal translation

Guantanamera: A lady
of Guantanamo
Guajira: Young woman

I'm a sincere man from
the land of palms. Before
dying, I wish to pour forth
the poems of my soul.

My verses are soft green but
also a flaming red. My
verses are like wounded
fauns seeking refuge in the
forest.

I want to share my fate with
the world's humble. A little
mountain stream pleases me
more than the ocean.

English lyrics

1. I'm just a man who is trying -
to do some good before dying,
To ask each man and his brother -
To bear no ill toward each other.
This life will never be hollow -
To those who listen and follow.

2. Guantanamera,
I write my rhymes to uncover -
My secret feelings, the rambling
thoughts of your lover.

Verse

I write my rhymes with no learning,
And yet with truth they are burning,
But 'is the world waiting for them?
Or will they all just ignore them?
Have I a poet's illusion,
A dream to die in seclusion? (Cho.)

3. Guantanamera, etc. (in Spanish)

Verse

A little brook on a mountain,
The cooling spray of a fountain -
Arouse in me an emotion, more
than the vast boundless ocean,
For there's a wealth beyond measure
In little things that we treasure.
(final Chorus, in Spanish)

Kiss of Fire

Registration 5
Rhythm: Tango or Latin

Words and Music by Lester Allen
and Robert Hill
(Adapted from A.G. Villoldo)

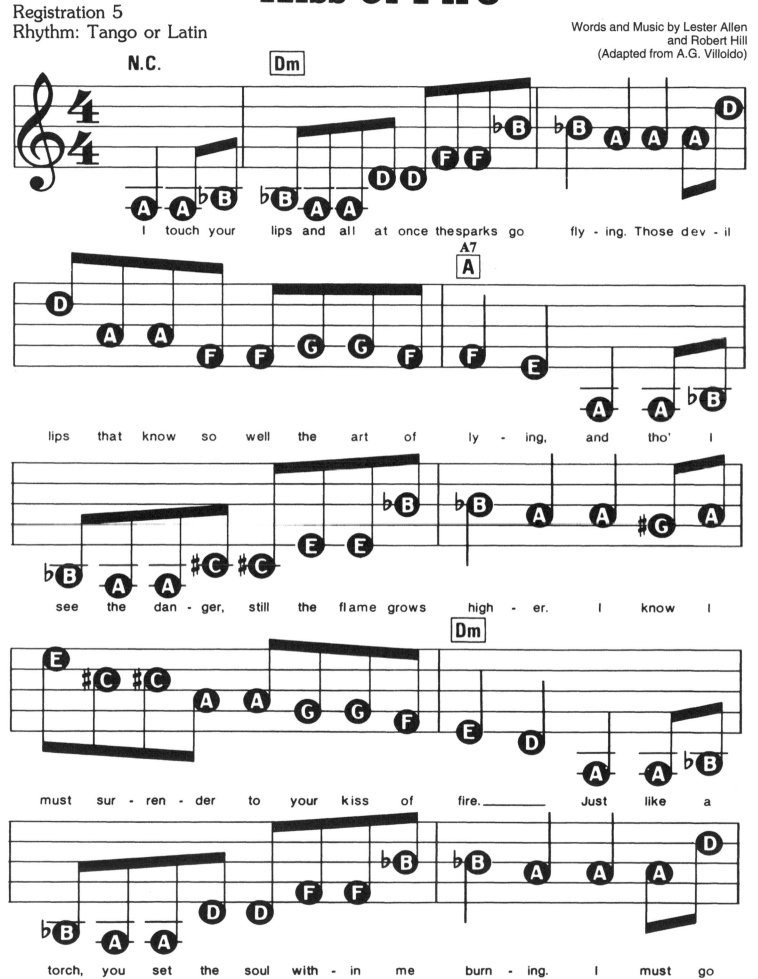

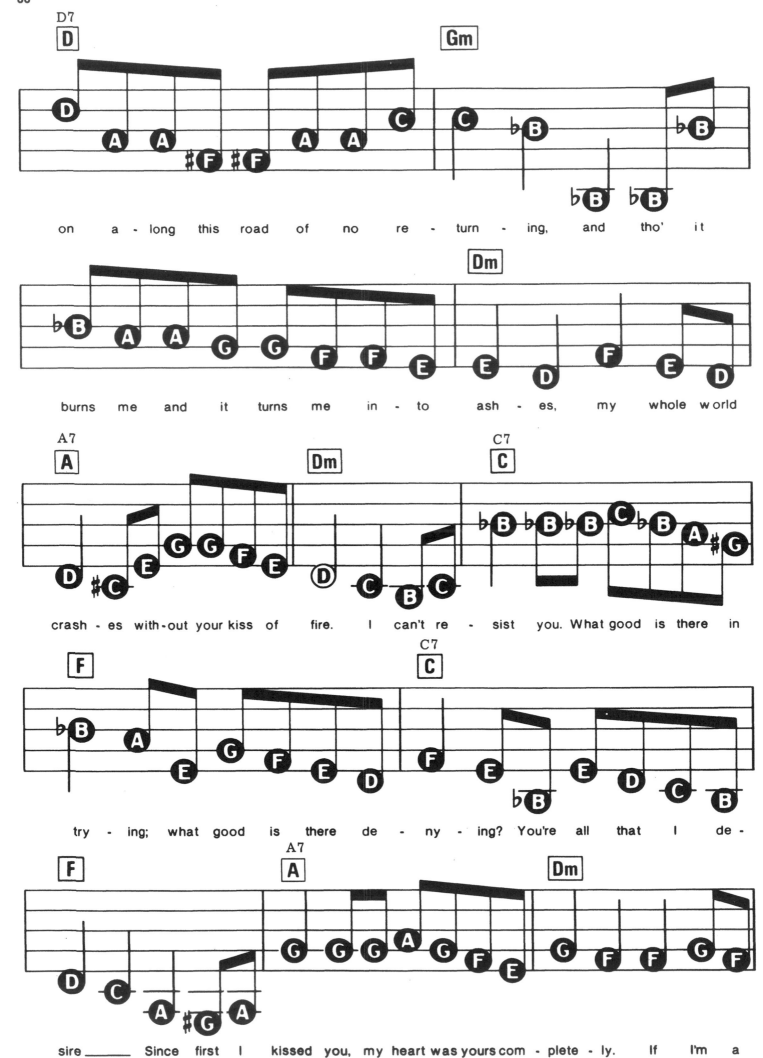

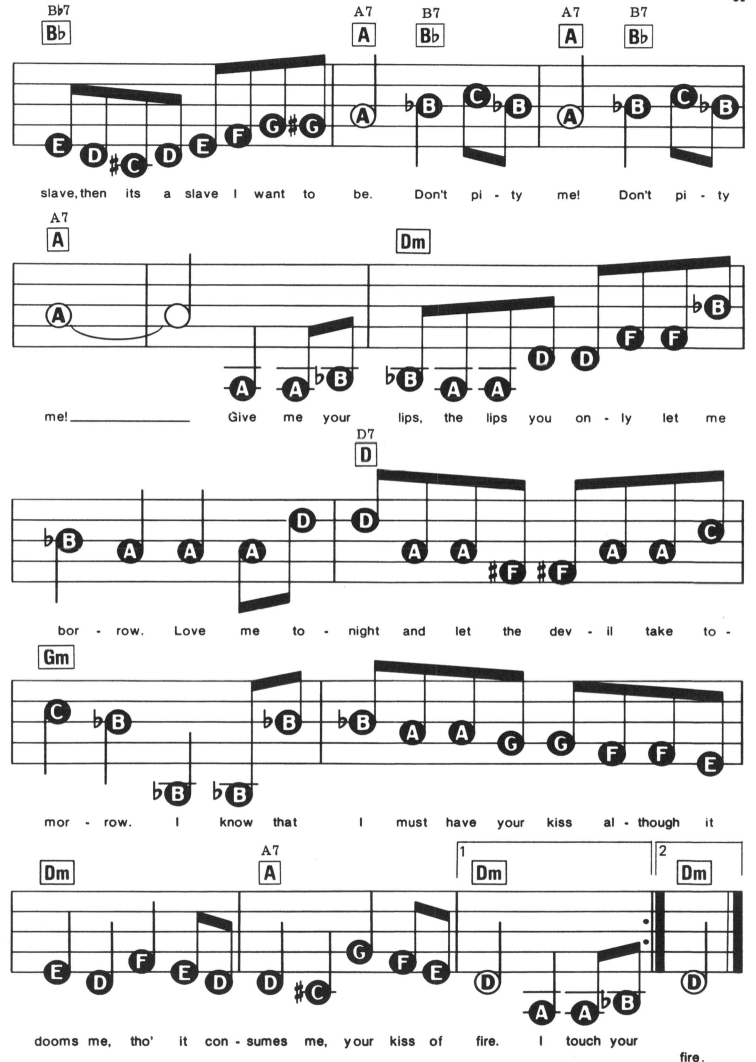

slave, then its a slave I want to be. Don't pi - ty me! Don't pi - ty

me! _____ Give me your lips, the lips you on - ly let me

bor - row. Love me to - night and let the dev - il take to -

mor - row. I know that I must have your kiss al - though it

dooms me, tho' it con - sumes me, your kiss of fire. I touch your

fire.

How Insensitive
(Insensatez)

Original Words by Vinicius de Moraes
English Words by Norman Gimbel
Music by Antonio Carlos Jobim

Registration 8
Rhythm: Bossa Nova or Latin

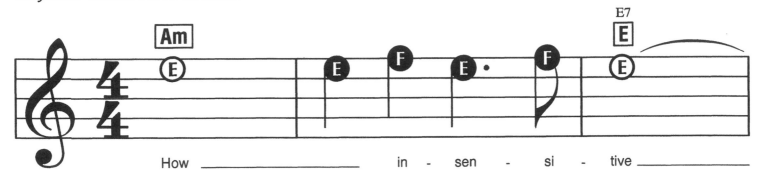

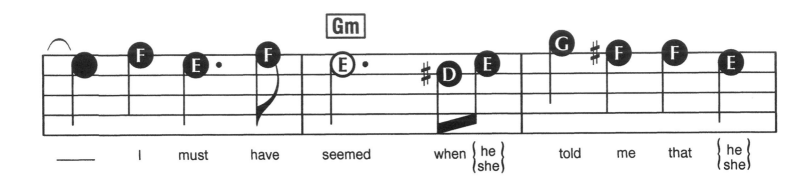

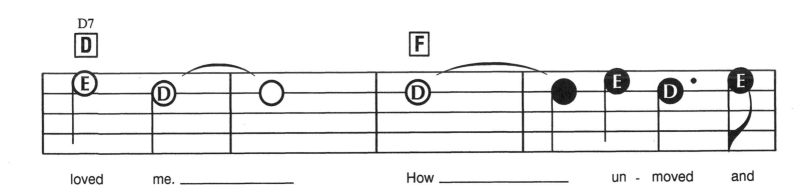

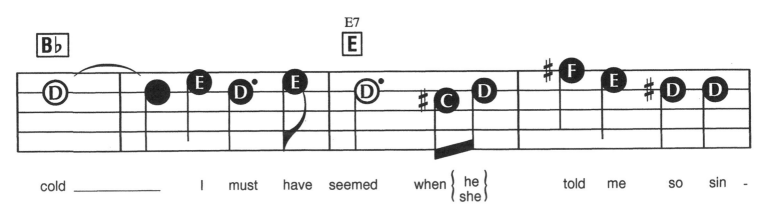

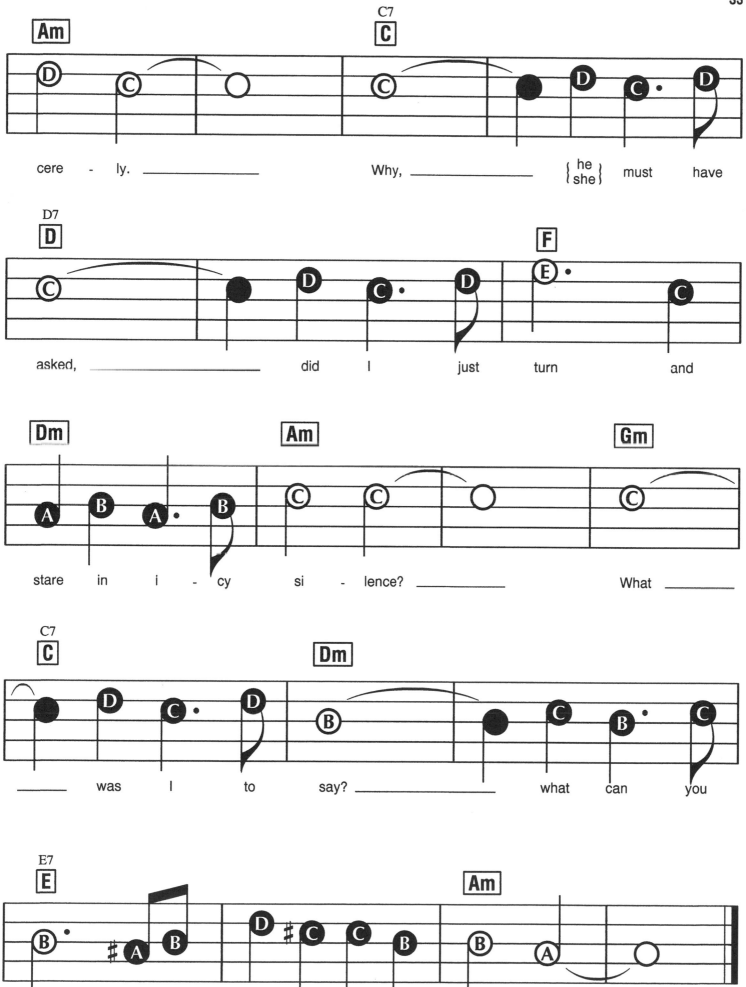

Mambo #5

Registration 1
Rhythm: Mambo or Latin

Words and Music by
Damaso Perez Prado

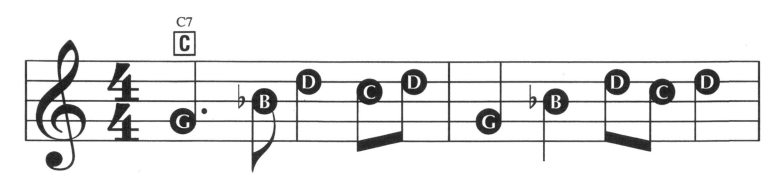

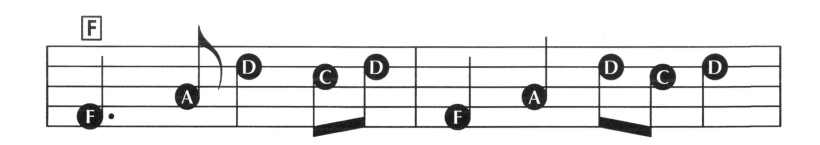

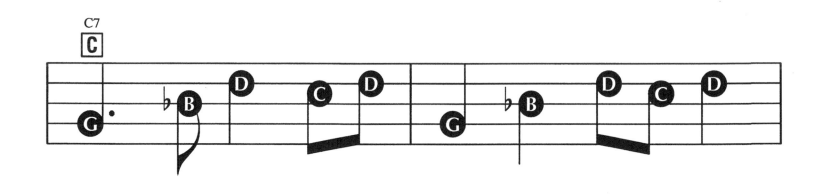

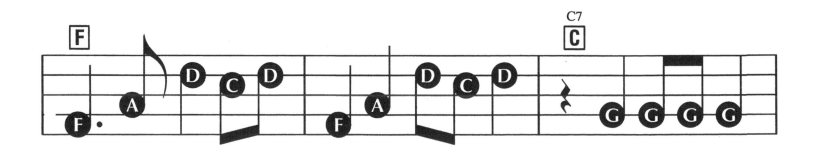

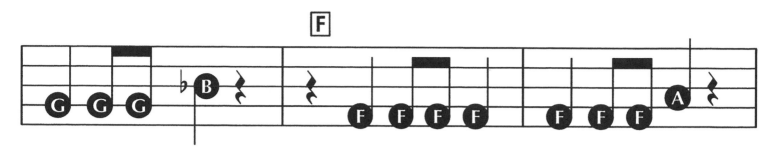

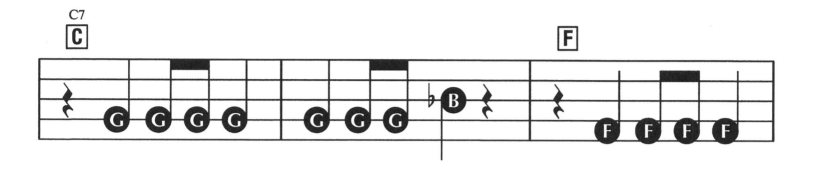

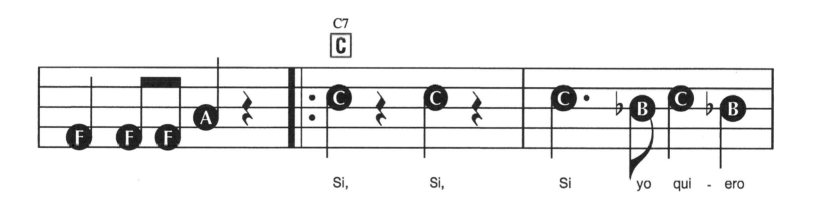

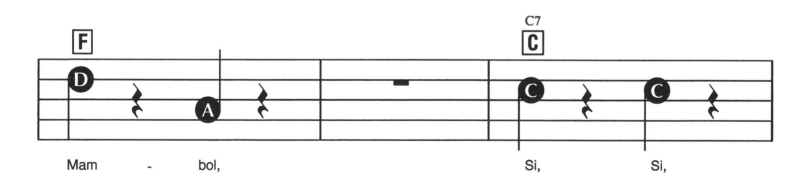

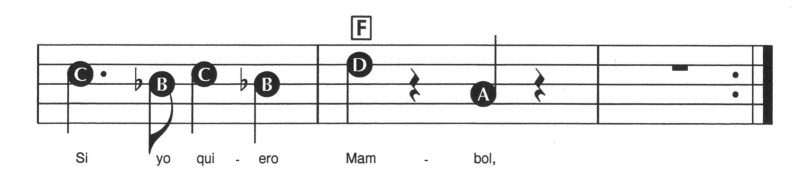

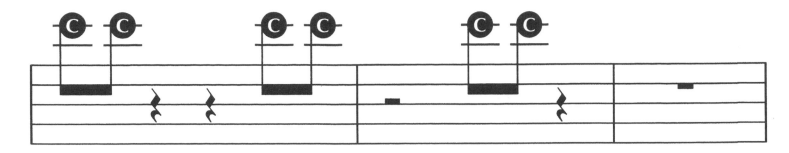

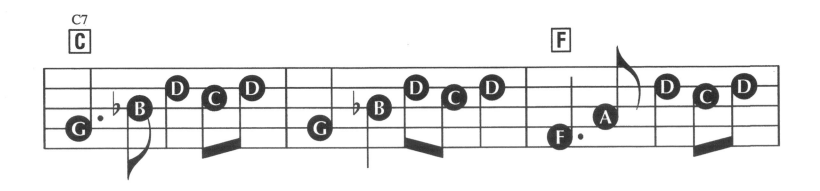

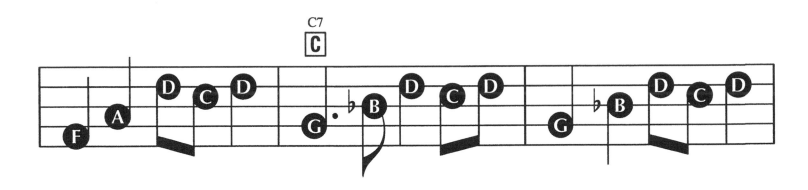

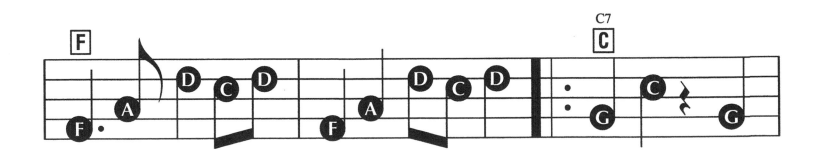

Repeat and Fade

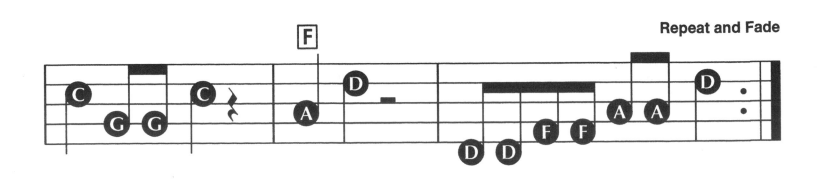

Miami Beach Rumba

Registration 3
Rhythm: Rhumba or Latin

Words by Albert Gamse
Music by Irving Fields

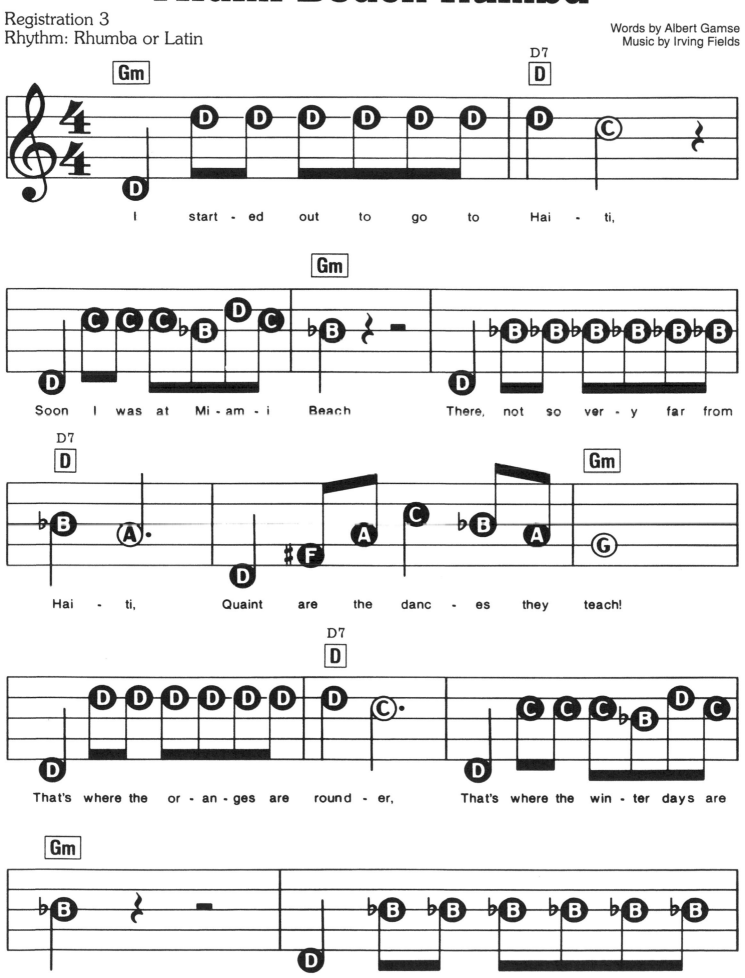

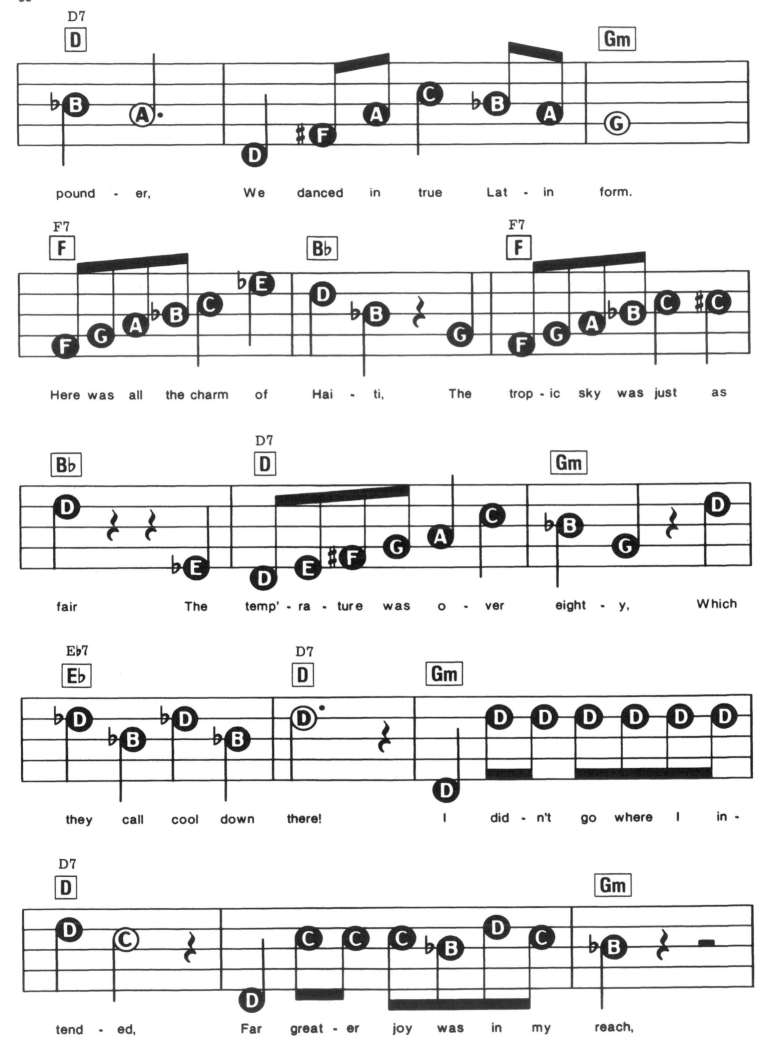

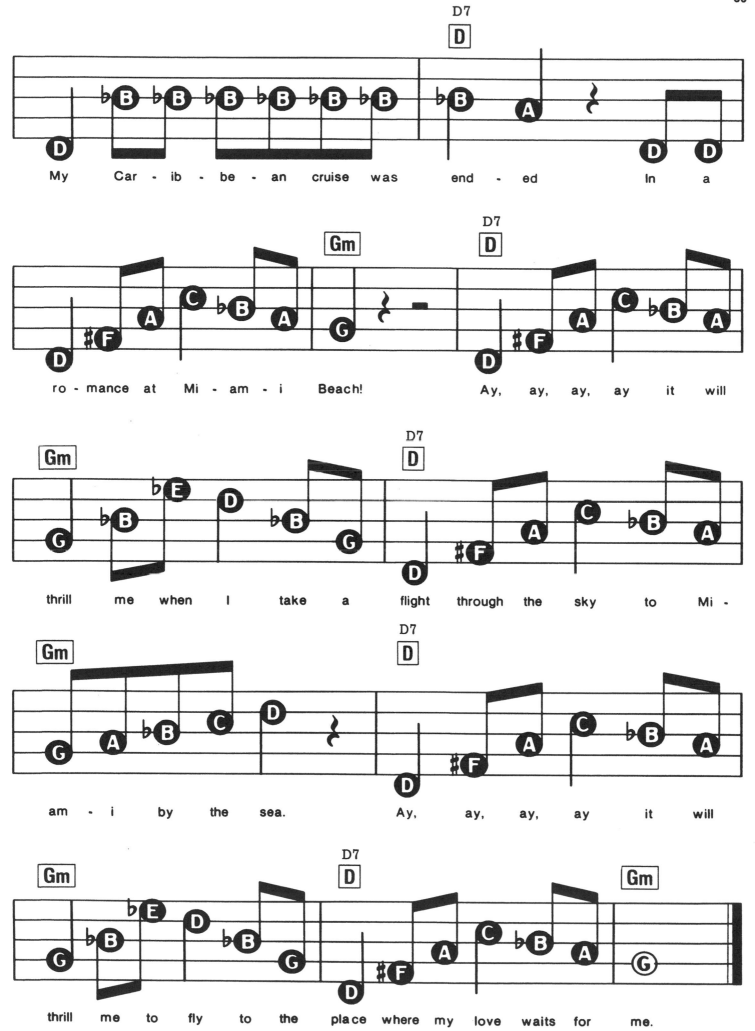

Maria Elena

Registration 10
Rhythm: Waltz

English Words by S.K. Russell
Music and Spanish Words by Lorenzo Barcelata

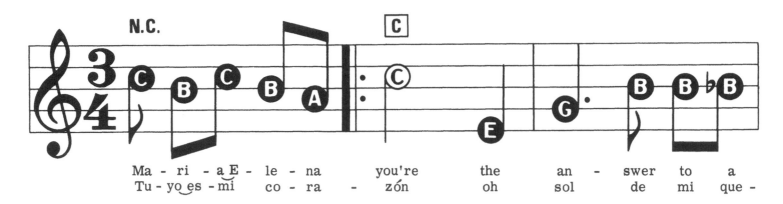

Ma - ri - a E - le - na   you're   the   an - swer to a
Tu - yo es - mi co - ra - zón   oh   sol   de mi que-

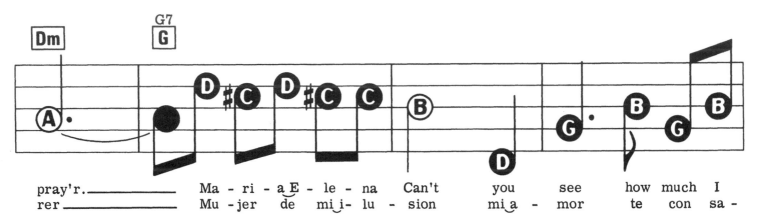

pray'r._____   Ma - ri - a E - le - na Can't   you   see   how much I
rer_____   Mu - jer de mi i - lu - sion   mi a - mor te con sa-

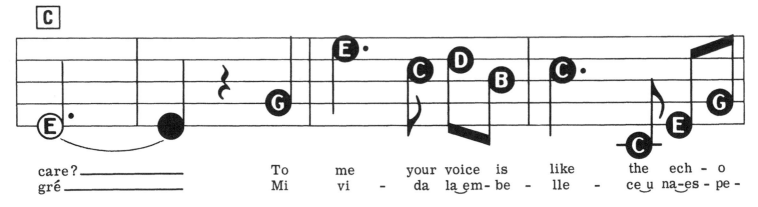

care?_____   To   me   your voice is   like   the ech - o
gré_____   Mi   vi - da la em - be - lle - ce u na - es - pe-

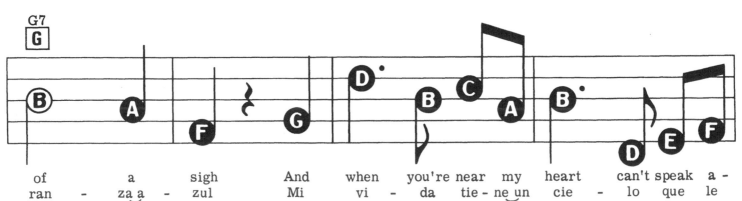

of   a   sigh   And   when   you're near my   heart   can't speak a-
ran - za a - zul   Mi   vi - da tie - ne un cie - lo que le

More
(Ti Guardero' Nel Cuore)
from the Film MONDO CANE

Registration 4
Rhythm: Latin or Bossa Nova

Music by Nino Oliviero and Riz Ortolani
Italian Words by Marcello Ciorciolini
English Words by Norman Newell

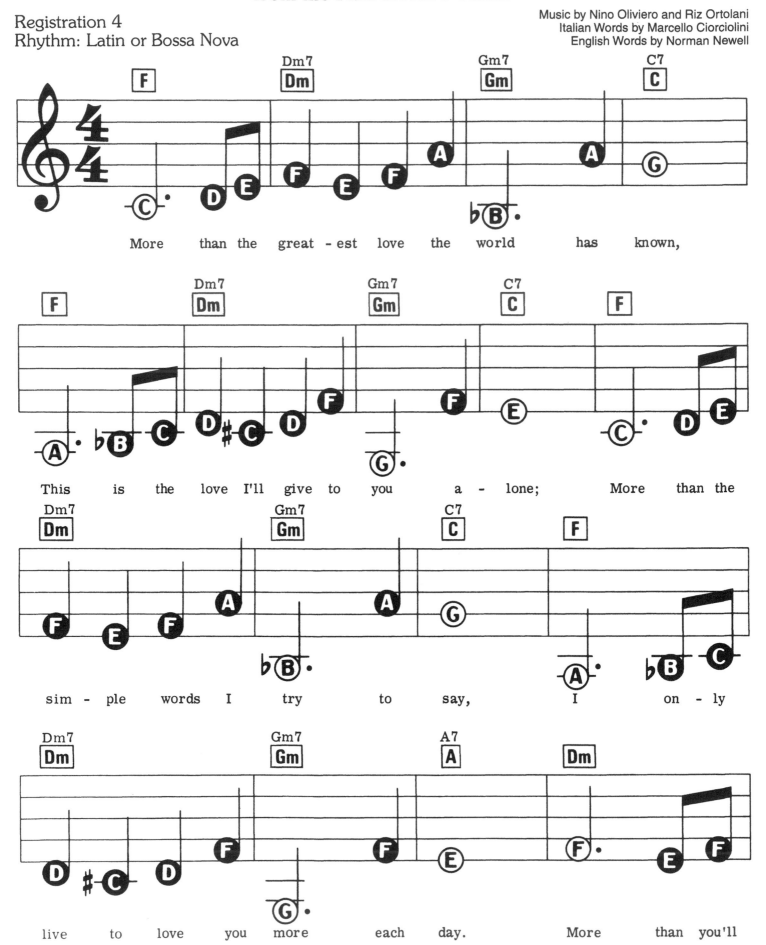

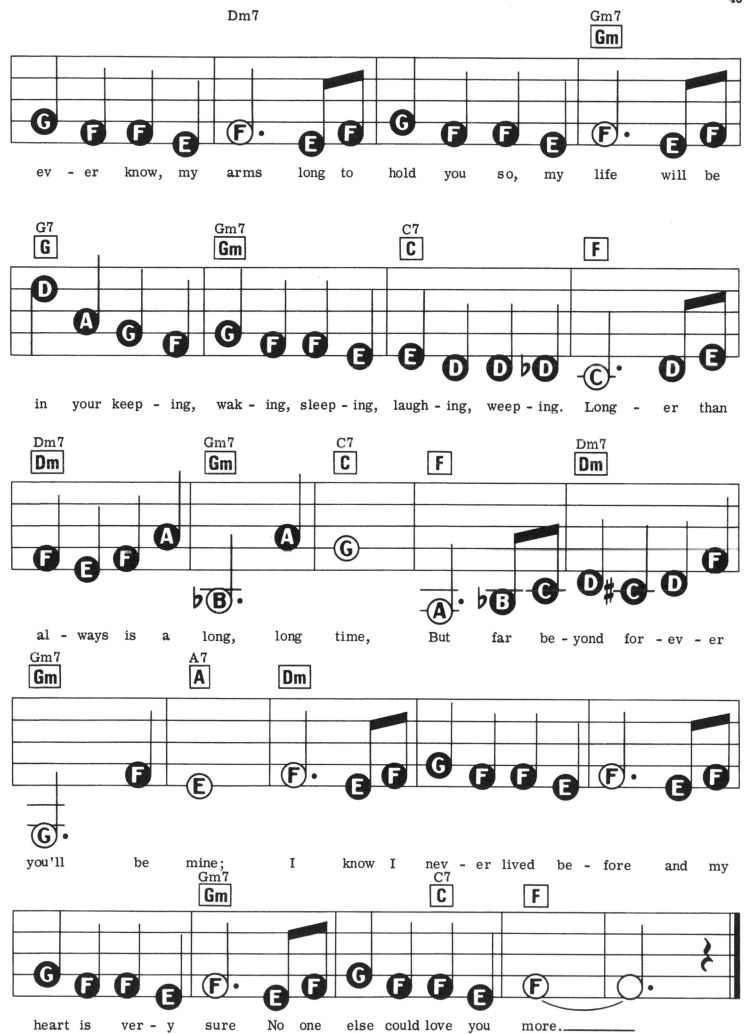

One Note Samba
(Samba De Uma Nota So)

Registration 8
Rhythm: Bossa Nova or Latin

Original Words by Newton Mendonca
English Words by Antonio Carlos Jobim
Music by Antonio Carlos Jobim

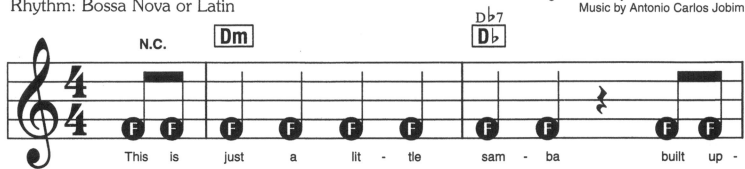

This is just a lit - tle sam - ba built up -

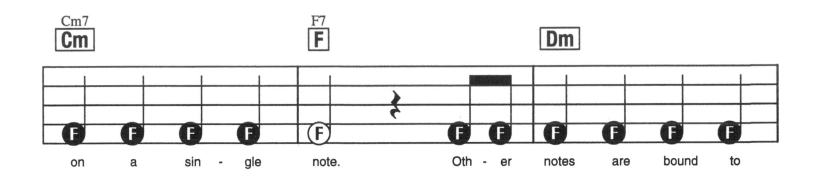

on a sin - gle note. Oth - er notes are bound to

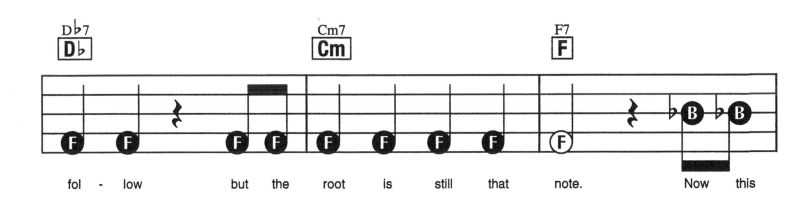

fol - low but the root is still that note. Now this

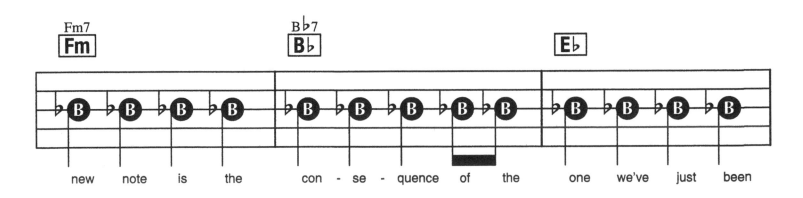

new note is the con - se - quence of the one we've just been

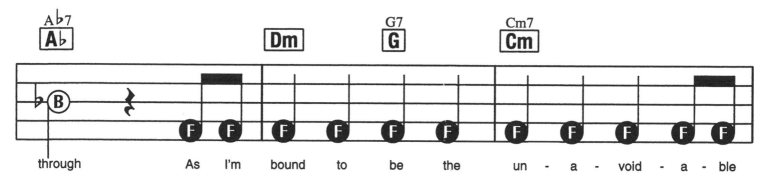

through As I'm bound to be the un - a - void - a - ble

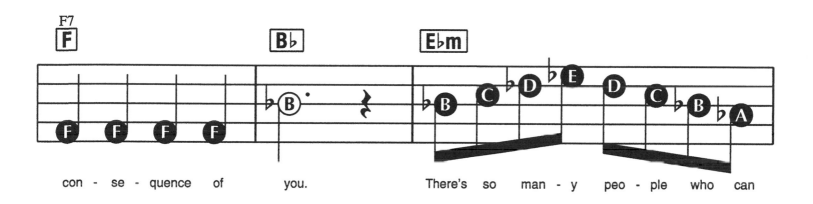

con - se - quence of you. There's so man - y peo - ple who can

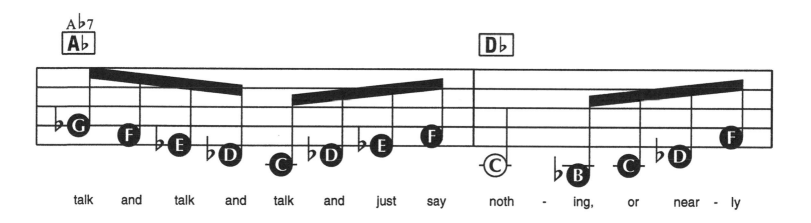

talk and talk and talk and just say noth - ing, or near - ly

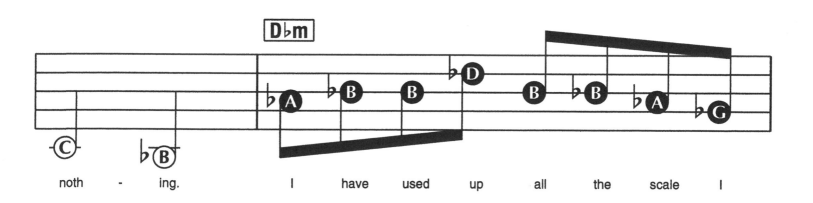

noth - ing. I have used up all the scale I

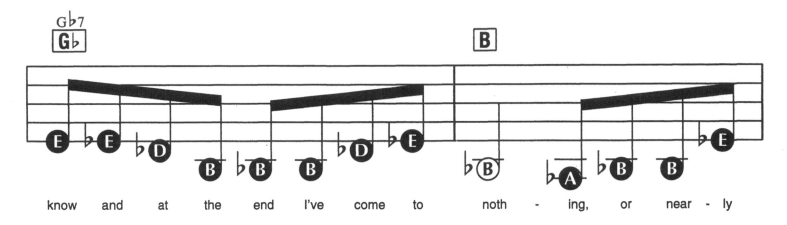

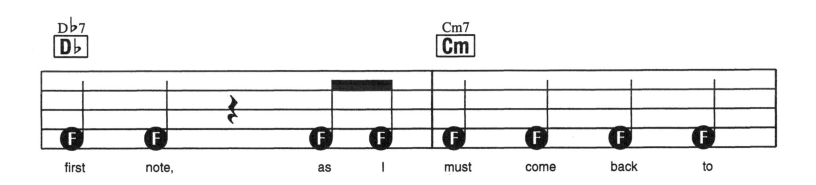

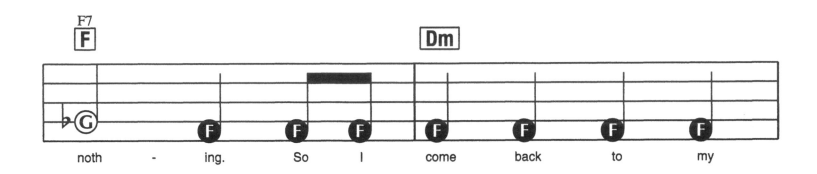

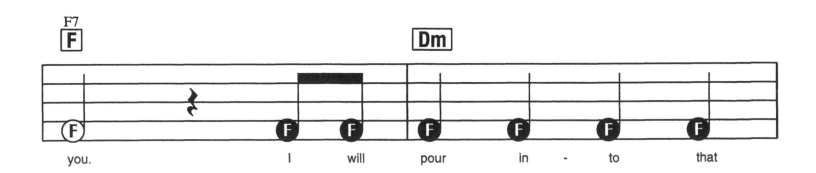

47

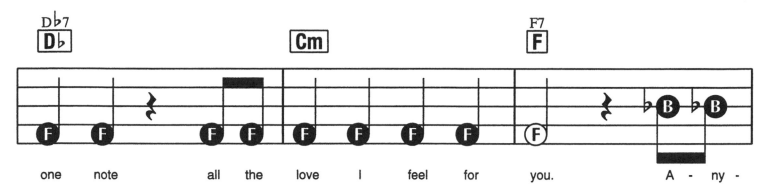

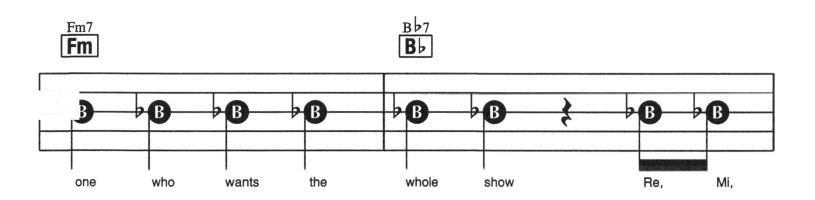

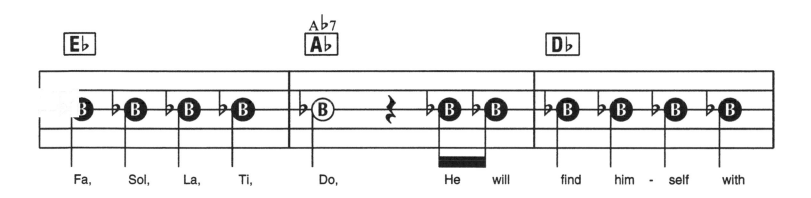

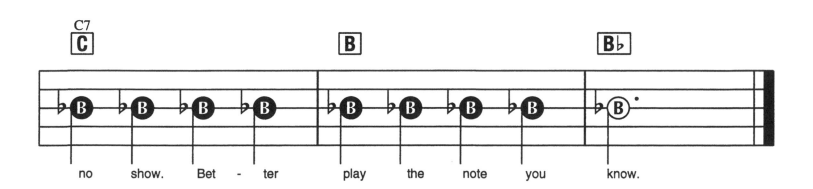

Perhaps, Perhaps, Perhaps
(Quizas, Quizas, Quizas)

Registration 4
Rhythm: Rhumba or Latin

Original Words and Music by Osvaldo Farres
English Words by Joe Davis

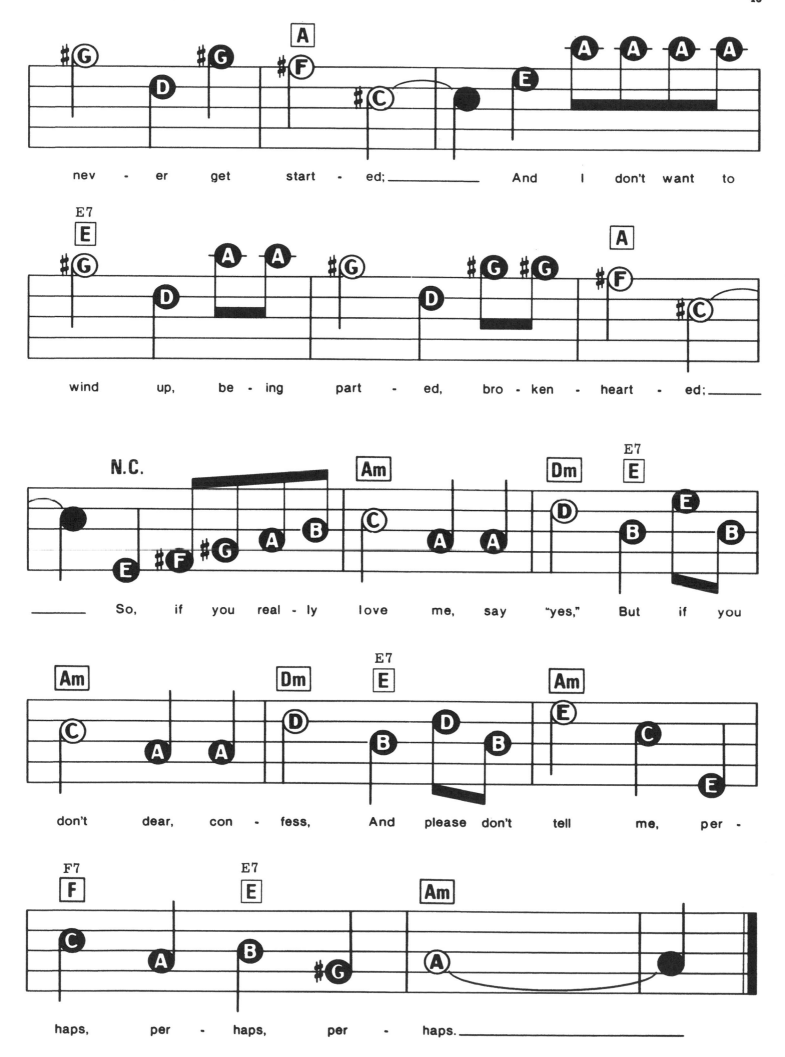

Poinciana
(Song of the Tree)

Registration 8
Rhythm: Rhumba or Latin

Words by Buddy Bernier
Music by Nat Simon

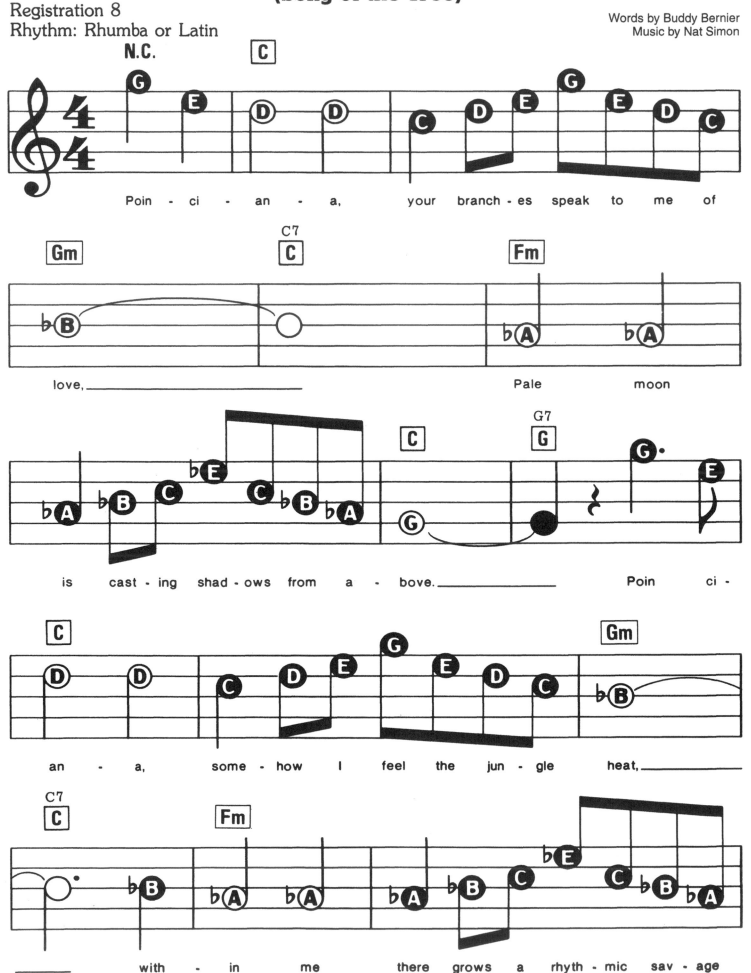

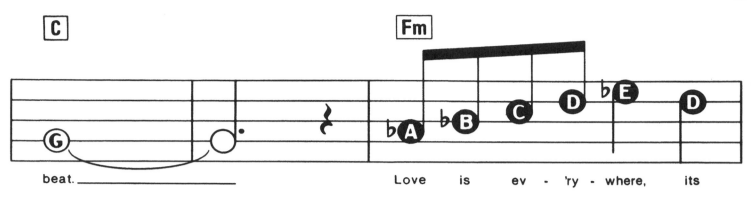

beat. _____ Love is ev - 'ry - where, its

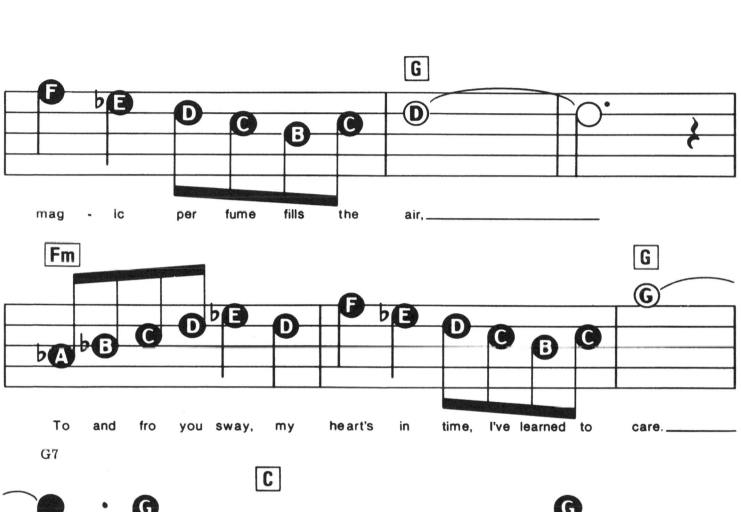

mag - ic per fume fills the air, _____

To and fro you sway, my heart's in time, I've learned to care. _____

G7

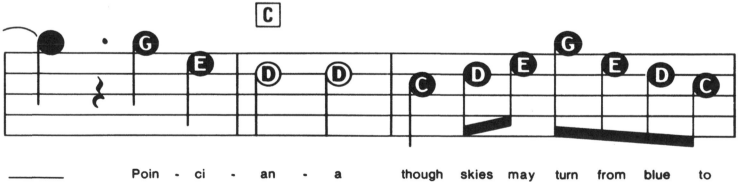

_____ Poin - ci - an - a though skies may turn from blue to

Gm   C7
      C   Fm

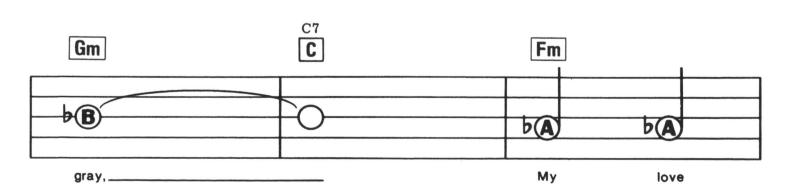

gray, _____ My love

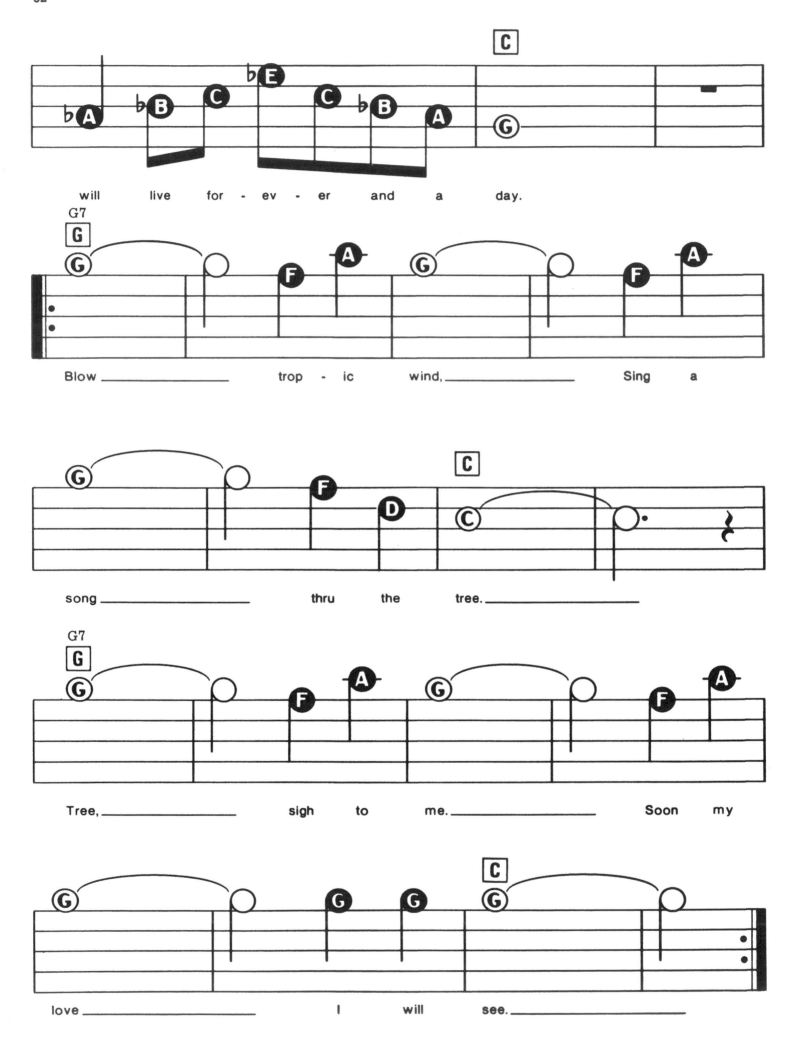

will live for - ev - er and a day.

Blow _____ trop - ic wind, _____ Sing a

song _____ thru the tree. _____

Tree, _____ sigh to me. _____ Soon my

love _____ I will see. _____

Spanish Eyes

Registration 3
Rhythm: Latin or Bossa Nova

Words by Charles Singleton and Eddie Snyder
Music by Bert Kaempfert

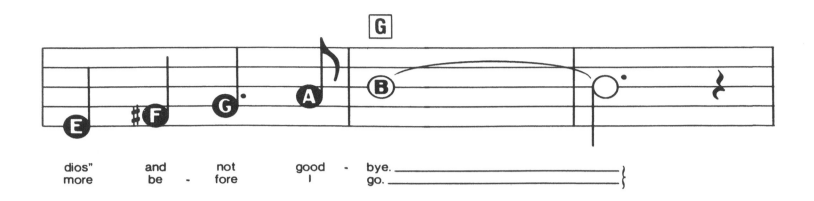

dios" and not good - bye. _____
more be - fore I go. _____ }

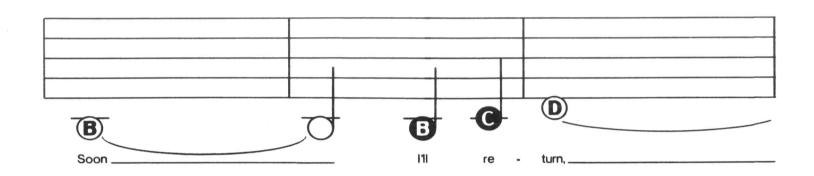

Soon _____ I'll re - turn, _____

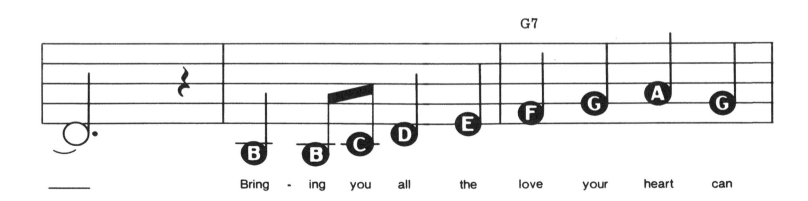

_____ Bring - ing you all the love your heart can

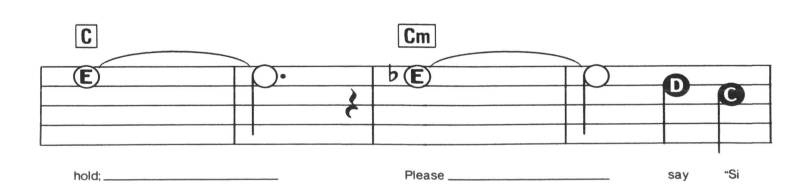

hold; _____ Please _____ say "Si

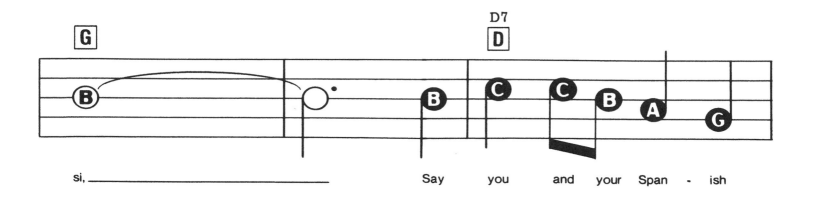

si, _____ Say you and your Span - ish

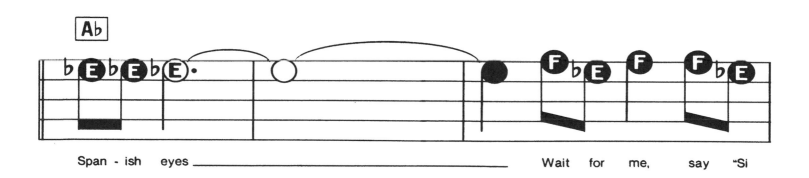

eyes will wait for me. _____

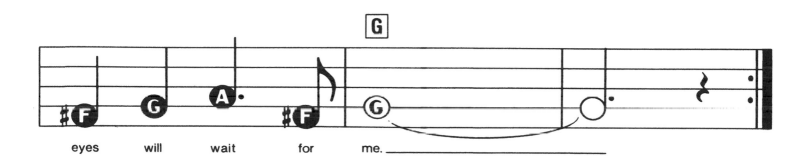

Span - ish eyes _____ Wait for me, say "Si

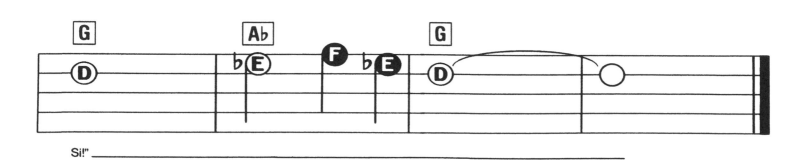

Si!" _____

Summer Samba

(So Nice)

Registration 4
Rhythm: Samba or Bossa Nova

Original Words and Music by Marcos Valle and Paulo Sergio Valle
English Words by Norman Gimbel

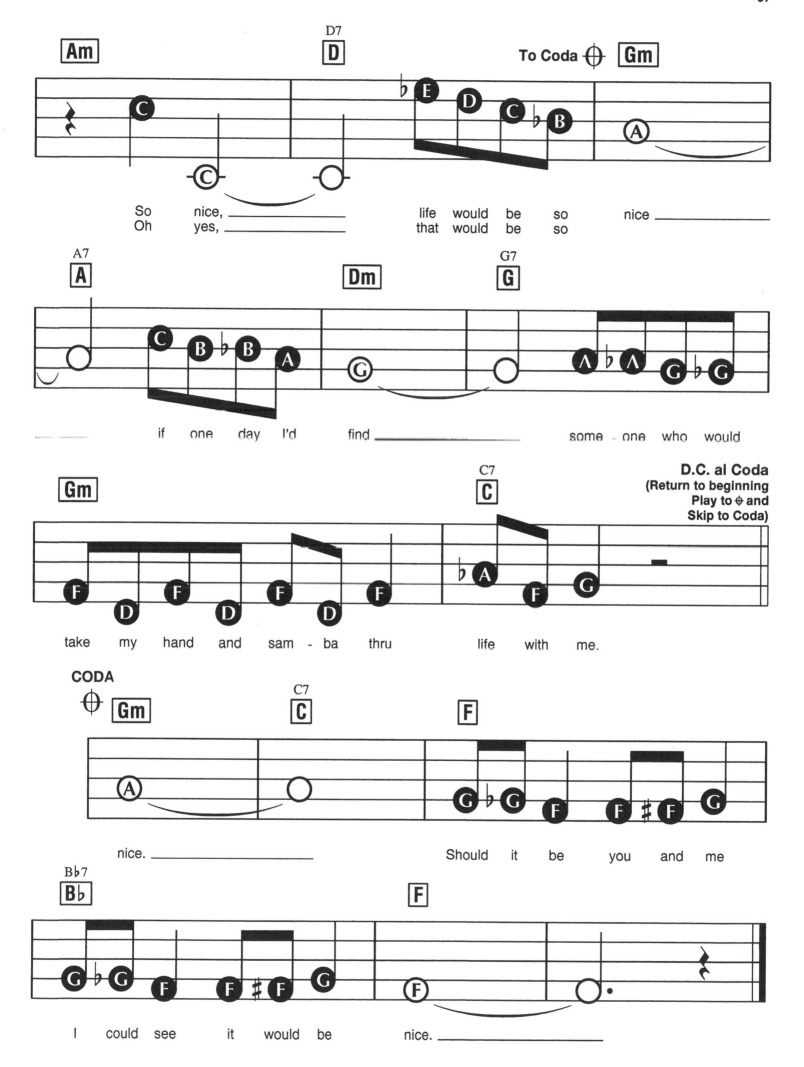

You Belong to My Heart
(Solamente Una Vez)

Registration 5
Rhythm: Rhumba or Latin

Original Words and Music by Agustin Lara
English Words by Ray Gilbert

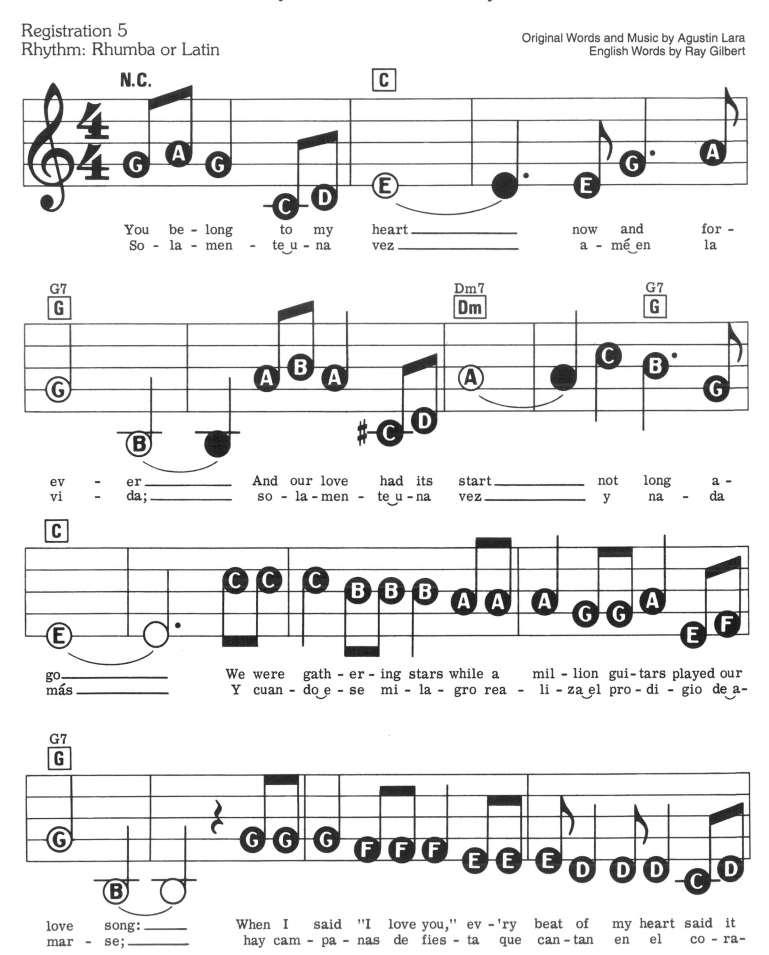

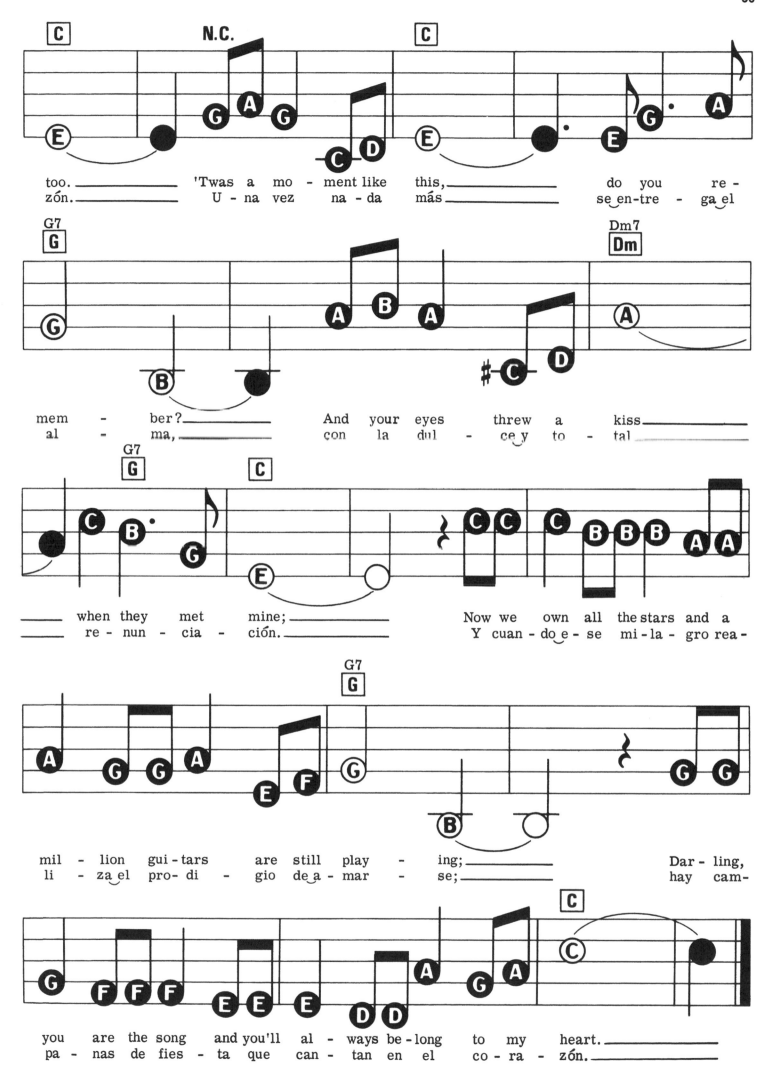

Yellow Days

Registration 1
Rhythm: Rhumba or Latin

English Words by Alan Bernstein
Music and Spanish Words by Alvaro Carrillo

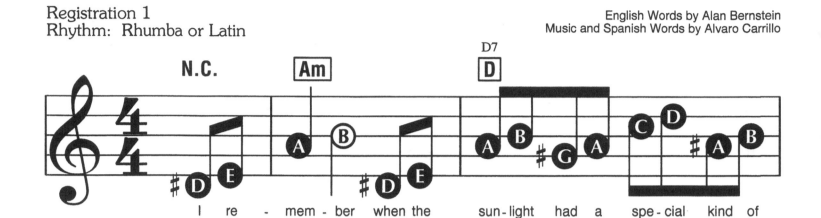

I re - mem - ber when the sun - light had a spe - cial kind of

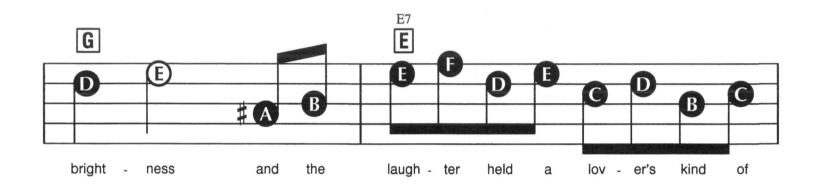

bright - ness and the laugh - ter held a lov - er's kind of

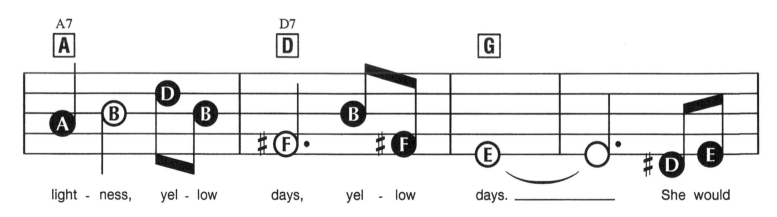

light - ness, yel - low days, yel - low days. _____ She would

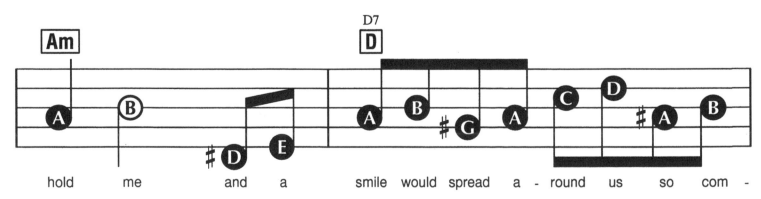

hold me and a smile would spread a - round us so com -

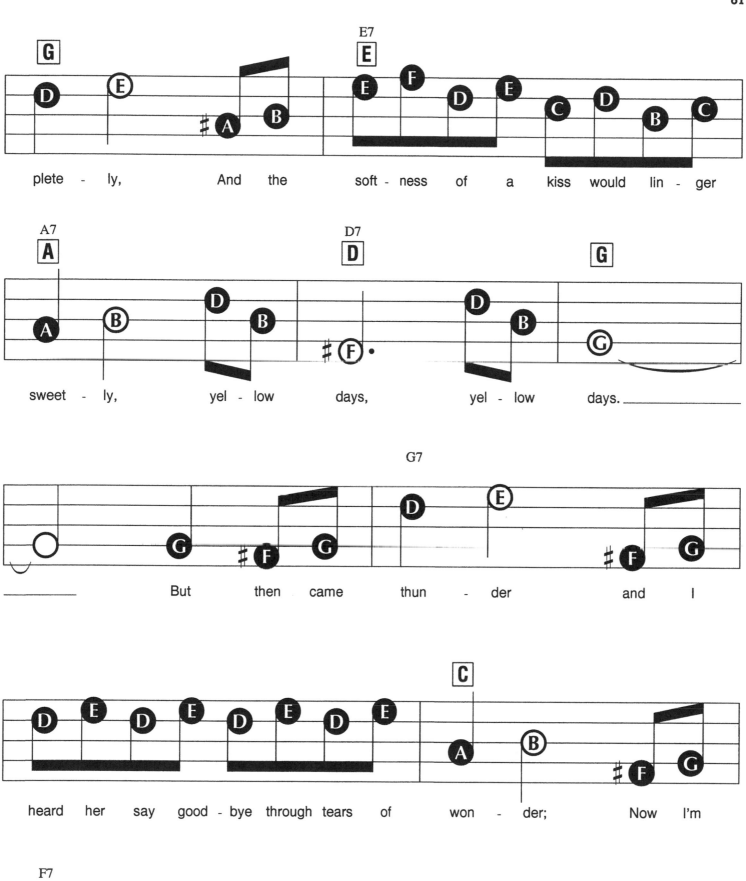

plete - ly, And the soft - ness of a kiss would lin - ger

sweet - ly, yel - low days, yel - low days. _____

_____ But then came thun - der and I

heard her say good - bye through tears of won - der; Now I'm

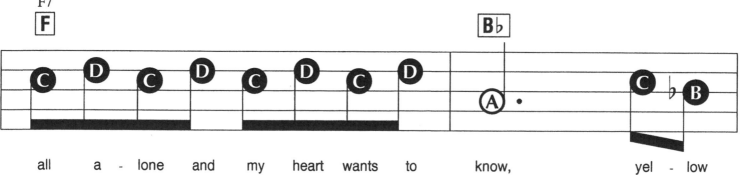

all a - lone and my heart wants to know, yel - low

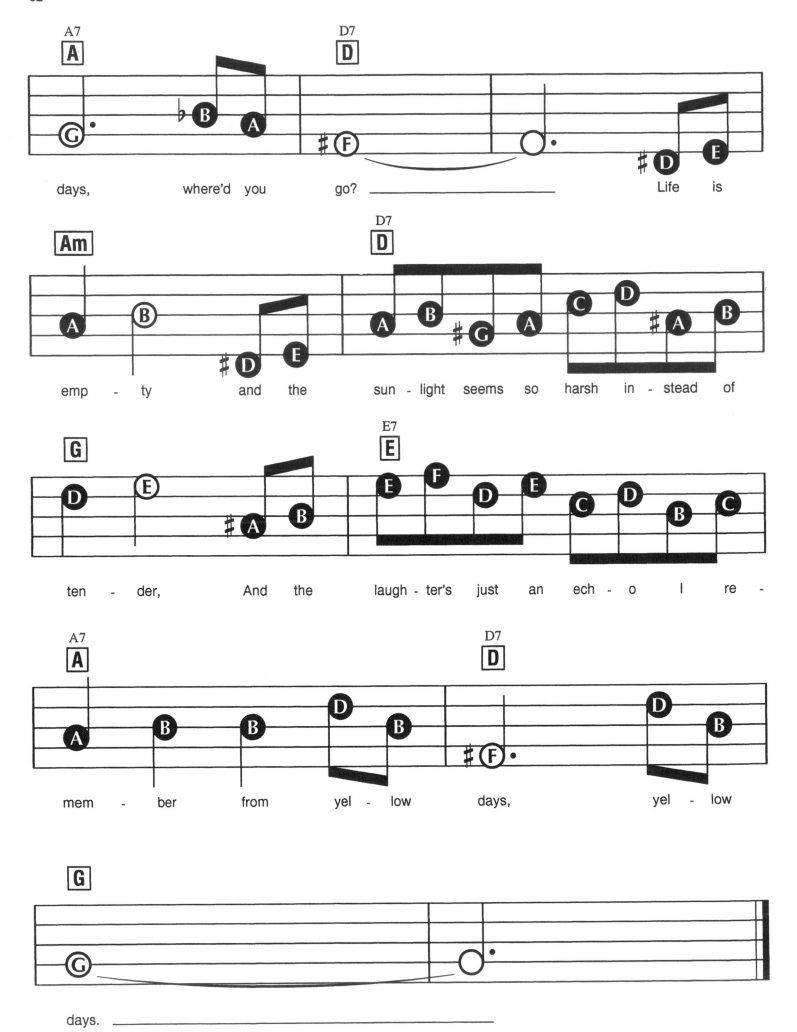

 **Registration Guide**

- Match the Registration number on the song to the corresponding numbered category below. Select and activate an instrumental sound available on your instrument.

- Choose an automatic rhythm appropriate to the mood and style of the song. (Consult your Owner's Guide for proper operation of automatic rhythm features.)

- Adjust the tempo and volume controls to comfortable settings.

Registration

1	Flutes, Clarinet, Oboe, Flugel Horn, Trombone, French Horn, Organ Flutes
2	Saxophones, Trumpet, Mute Trumpet, Synth Leads, Jazz/Gospel Organs
3	Acoustic/Electric Guitars, Banjo, Mandolin, Dulcimer, Ukulele, Hawaiian Guitar
4	Violin, Viola, Cello, Fiddle, String Ensemble, Pizzicato, Organ Strings
5	Vibraphone, Marimba, Xylophone, Steel Drums, Bells, Celesta, Chimes
6	Accordion, French Accordion, Mussette, Harmonica, Pump Organ, Bagpipes
7	Pipe Organ, Hand Bells, Vocal Ensemble, Choir, Organ Flutes
8	Piano, Electric Piano, Honky Tonk Piano, Harpsichord, Clavi
9	Melodic Percussion, Wah Trumpet, Synth, Whistle, Kazoo, Perc. Organ
10	Bass Section, Sax Section, Wind Ensemble, Full Organ, Theater Organ